A PASSION FOR RADIO

A PASSION FOR RADIO

Radio Waves and Community

Edited by Bruce Girard

An AMARC Project

Montréal/New York

BLACK ROSE BOOKS No. V178
Hardcover ISBN: 1-895431-35-2
Paperback ISBN: 1-895431-34-4
Library of Congress Catalog No. 92-072627

Canadian Cataloguing in Publication Data

Main entry under title:

A Passion for Radio: radio waves and community

ISBN: 1-895431-35-2 (bound) ISBN: 1-895431-34-4 (pbk.)

1. Radio broadcasting. 2. Radio in community development.

3. Local mass media. I. Girard, Bruce

HE8S96.P37 1992 3B4.54 C92-090358-4

Cover Design: Werner Arnold
Cover Illustration: Michel Granger

The publication of this book was made possible with the help of the Fondation pour le Progrès de l'Homme (France), the Canadian Catholic Organisation for Development and Peace, and the Canadian International Development Agency (CIDA).

This book is published in French under the title *La Passion Radio,* Éditions Syros (France) and in Spanish under the title *Radiopasionados* by CIESPAL (Ecuador).

General coordination was carried out by Bruce Girard with the collaboration of Evelyne Foy of AMARC. Thanks to the many writers and collaborators without whom this book would not have been possible.

Mailing Address

BLACK ROSE BOOKS
C.P. 1258
Succ. Place du Parc
Montréal, Québec
H2W 2R3 Canada

BLACK ROSE BOOKS
340 Nagel Drive
Cheektowaga, New York
14225 USA

A publication of the Institute of Policy Alternatives of Montéal (IPAM)

Printed in Canada

Table of Contents

Notes on AMARC

THE WORLD ASSOCIATION OF COMMUNITY RADIO BROADCASTERS

Known by its French acronym, AMARC, the World Association of Community Radio broadcasters is an international organization serving the community radio movement. It is a network for exchange and solidarity among community broadcasters and its work involves consulting, coordinating and facilitating cooperation and exchange among community radio broadcasters worldwide. AMARC's goal is to support and contribute to the development of community radio along the principles of solidarity and international understanding. AMARC's Declaration of Principles states, in part, that members of AMARC:

- believe in the need to establish a new world information order based on more just and equitable exchanges among peoples;
- contribute to the expression of different social, political and cultural movements, and to the promotion of all initiatives supporting peace, friendship among peoples, democracy and development;
- recognize the fundamental and specific role of women in establishing new communication practices;
- express through their programming: the sovereignty and independence of all peoples; solidarity and non-intervention in the internal affairs of other countries; international cooperation based on the creation of permanent and widespread ties based on equality, reciprocity, and mutual respect; non-discrimination on the basis of race, sex, sexual preference or religion; and respect for the cultural identity of peoples.

* * *

AMARC's head office is located at 3575 boulevard St-Laurent, suite 704, Montréal, Québec, Canada H2X 2T7. Telephone: +(514) 982-0351. Fax: +(514) 849-7129.

Latin American regional office: c/o CEPES, 818 avenida Salaberry, Jesús María, Lima, Peru. Telephone: +(51) 14-237-884. Fax: +(51) 14-331-744.

In Africa, AMARC works closely with the Centre interafricain d'étude en radio rurale de Ouagadougou (CIERRO) B.P. 385, Ouagadougou, Burkina Faso. Telephone: +(226) 30-66-86. Fax: +(226) 31-28-66.

Contributors

Tachi Arriola is a member of Peru's Feminist Radio Collective with many years of experience in popular communication in Peru.

Eugénie Aw is a Senegalese journalist and one of the founders of the Association des Professionelles de la Communication (APAC). She is the coordinator of AMARC's African activities.

Richard Barette is the former head of French-language programming at Radio Centre-Ville in Montréal.

Pascal Bergué is head of research in the communication department of the Groupe de Recherche et d'échanges techniques (GRET). He is based in Paris.

Louise Boivin is a former news director of Radio Centreville in Montréal, Québec. She is currently coordinating the station's *Ondes de Femmes* project.

Arturo Bregaglio is a member of CECOPAL (Centro de Comunicación Popular y Asesoramiento Legal) and Radio FM Sur in Cordoba, Argentina.

MJR David is a former producer with Sri Lanka's Mahaweli Community Radio. He has a degree in Development Communication from the University of Philippines.

Richard Chateau-Dégat is a professor and president of the Association for the Development of Grassroots Communication, the organization that manages Martinique's Radio Asé Pléré An Nou Lité.

Michel Delorme is coordinator of the rural radio program of the Association de Cooperation Culturelles et Techniques. He is a founder and president of AMARC. He has worked extensively with community radio in Québec and Canada.

Isabelle Fortin is former journalist at Montréal's Radio Centre-Ville. She currently lives in Haiti where she is involved in a project to develop a rural radio network.

Evelyne Foy is Secretary General of AMARC. She has worked extensively with Québec's community radio stations, including Radio Centre-Ville.

Joseph Georges is former Program Director of Radio Soleil in Port au Prince, Haiti and a member of AMARC's Board of Directors. He is currently working towards developing a network of rural community radio stations in Haiti.

Bruce Girard has worked in community radio projects in North America, Latin America and Europe. He is one of the founders of AMARC and former editor of the association's bulletin, *InteRadio.*

Edric Gorfinkel is founder and coordinator of CASET. He has worked as a teacher in Ecuador, the United States and Zimbabwe and as a radio and television broadcaster in Zimbabwe.

Barbara Kent works with Mediaconsult, an international consulting firm with offices in Czechoslovakia and the United States.

Dorothy Kidd has worked at Co-op Radio since 1980, both as a volunteer and a staff member. She has researched popular communications in Canada and India and is currently completing her Ph.D. at Simon Fraser University in Vancouver.

Serguei Korzoun is Radio Echo of Moscow's news director. He formerly worked for the French-language service of Radio Moscow International.

Francois Laureys is a former volunteer with Radio 100. He now works as a journalist with the state radio network

Eric L'oiseau produces a jazz program at Radio Centre-Ville.

José Ignacio López has extensive experience training for popular radio in Latin America. He has written several books about radio. He is coordinator of AMARC's Latin American office.

Lavinia Mohr is a former station manager and long-time programmer at Vancouver Cooperative Radio and one of the founders of AMARC. She immigrated from the United States to Canada in 1975 and currently resides in Toronto where she works for a community development agency active in ten countries.

Stanislav Perkner works with Mediaconsult, an international consulting firm with offices in Czechoslovakia and the United States.

Anna Leah Sarabia is founder and coordinator of the Women's Media Circle in Manila, the Philippines.

Ron Sakolsky was involved with WTRA/Zoom Black Magic Liberation Radio from the start, doing a weekly African/Caribbean/hip hop show. He teaches at Springfield's Sangamon State University. He is a member of the Union for Democratic Communications and a national board member of the Alliance for Cultural Democracy.

Sergio Tagle is a member of CECOPAL (Centro de Comunicación Popular y Asesoramiento Legal) and Radio FM Sur.

Bill Thomas is director of Pacifica Program Services in Los Angeles and a member of AMARC's Board of Directors.

Eduardo Valenzuela is an anthropologist and Deputy Director of the Radio Department at Mexico's Instituto Nacional Indigenista. He is also a member of AMARC's Board of Directors.

Preface

A Network of International Exchange

Many groups and individuals around the world have discovered that radio allows them to gain control of a genuine communication tool that encourages creativity and allows popular access. Daily, from one end of the planet to the other, communication enthusiasts manage to make radio a collective enterprise devoted to development.

This is not a utopia, or the dream of a few marginalised people — it is a phenomenon taking place on every continent. People are coming together to make the airwaves a real public place. The most widespread medium in many countries, and easily accessible following a minimal training period, community radio restores radio's vocation as an instrument of two-way communication.

Community radio goes by many names. It is called popular or educational radio in Latin America, rural or local radio in Africa, public radio in Australia and free or associative radio in Europe. All these names describe the same phenomenon: that of gaining a voice and democratizing communication on a community scale.

Community radio, although taking on diverse forms depending on its surroundings, remains a type of radio made to serve people; radio that encourages expression and participation and that values local culture. Its purpose is to give a voice to those without voices, to marginalised groups and to communities far from large urban centres, where the population is too small to attract commercial or large-scale State radio.

The World Association of Community Radio Broadcasters, AMARC, is an international non-governmental organization serving the community radio movement and uniting community radio workers from the five continents.

A network of exchange and solidarity, AMARC is also an association for consultation, coordination, cooperation and promotion of community radio. Through the association, new links are created, allowing everyone to learn of each others practices and experiences. Much like neurons forming a circuit, each unit is a centre which can freely communicate with the other units: acting locally, we are thinking globally. Community broadcasters form an open network in constant transformation.

The spirit which drives AMARC is geared toward encouraging direct exchange between the groups who use radio in their communities, as much in the North as in the South. We are convinced that communication is at the heart of the process of self-development of communities and that radio can amplify efforts at local, national and international levels, in order for those concerned to take control of development.

Community radio is dedicated to advancement. It must become a counterbalance to the concentration of media power in the hands of a few and the homogenization of cultural content. Community radio broadcasting offers an alternative for internal development. Speaking out is a synonym for taking control, and this is what, with passion, radio lovers are contributing to all over the world!

* * *

Michel Delorme
President of AMARC

1

Introduction

Bruce Girard

> *Radio could be the most wonderful public communication system imaginable... if it were capable, not only of transmitting, but of receiving, of making the listener not only hear but also speak.*
>
> — Bertolt Brecht, 1932

A PASSION FOR RADIO

In a world where information was the preserve of the literate urban minority with access to newspapers and books, the first regular radio broadcasts of the 1920's made it possible to imagine that the medium might really become the "wonderful public communication system" envisioned by Brecht. Radio did in fact bring about a radical transformation in the nature of social communication. Often this transformation was democratic, but it had its dark side as well. Little more than a decade after the first radio stations went on the air, Adolf Hitler made effective use of radio to propel himself to power.

Radio developed in very different ways in different parts of the world. In the United States, competition and commercialism were the rule. In Europe and its colonies, radio operated under centralized State control. In Canada, a combination of the two gave birth to a system with a strong centralized State network on the national level and competition and commercialism on the local level. And Latin America developed a radiophonic salad of State, private, church, university, special interest and indigenous peoples radio stations.

As time went on, the models blended and changed. Commercial radio appeared first in western and later eastern Europe. Public radio became a part of the media environment in the United States. In Africa, many of the national networks are in the process of decentralizing, adopting new objectives such as development, education and community participation.

However, as we near the end of the century, radio appears to be in decline. Eclipsed by other media, radio is overlooked in public policy debates and often neglected in the plans and budgets of both State broadcasting networks and media corporations. And rather than engaging its audience as Brecht had hoped, it has become predominantly concerned with its search for larger audiences. In much of the world, the majority of radio stations either choose to make their programming as bland as possible in the hope that they will attract listeners by not offending anyone, or they adopt sensationalist programming, hoping to attract listeners by offending everyone.

So, why a "passion for radio"? The answer to that question is found in a third type of radio — an alternative to commercial and State radio. Often referred to as *community radio,* its most distinguishing characteristic is its commitment to community participation at all levels. While listeners of commercial radio are able to participate in the programming in limited ways — via open line telephone shows or by requesting a favourite song, for example — community radio listeners are the producers, managers, directors, evaluators and even the owners of the stations.

This alternative form of radio is becoming increasingly important for those at the margins of society, those who seek political and cultural change. From the native-owned *Wawatay Radio Network* in northern Canada, to *Radio Venceremos,* operated by Salvadorean revolutionaries, to the rural station in the Kayes region of Mali, alternative and community radio stations fulfil an essential role for the outcasts of commercial and large-scale State media. Women, indigenous peoples, ethnic and linguistic minorities, youth, the political left, peasants, national liberation movements, and others are discovering the potential of radio as a means of political and cultural intervention and development. They are transforming radio into a medium that serves their needs — a medium that allows them to speak as well as hear.

This radio is not filled with pop music and "easy listening" newscasts, nor with official communiqués or government-sanctioned cultural content. It is not so important that the programming be "slick," but that it be based on a concept of participatory communication. The role of the radio is to respond to the priorities set by the community, to facilitate their discussion, to reinforce them, and to challenge them. Juggling all the interests of a community is difficult, and community radio does not always succeed. However, when it does, its broadcasts are marked with a passion rarely seen in commercial or large-scale State media. This passion arises out of a desire to empower listeners by encouraging and enabling their participation, not only in the radio but in the social, cultural and political processes that affect the community.

A WIDE RANGE OF COMMUNITY RADIO PROJECTS

The primary objective of this book is to present a wide range of community radio projects, not so that the "ideal" model can be identified, but in the hope that the book will serve as a useful tool for community broadcasters and potential community broadcasters looking to create or adapt models of community radio that are suited to the specific conditions they face. This objective of facilitating an international exchange of experiences and ideas has been AMARC's primary motivator since the first World Conference of Community Radio Broadcasters took place in 1983.

The use of radio as a tool for cultural and political change, while a growing phenomena, is not new. Indeed, the first participatory community radio stations surfaced almost simultaneously in Colombia and the United States over forty years ago. Since that time, innumerable participatory radio projects have attempted to promote community-led change in a variety of ways.

Some of these projects have attempted to foster this change by providing formal education in areas such as literacy and mathematics, or by promoting agricultural techniques suited to a particular vision of development defined by the central government. This type of project has been common in the Third World, especially in Africa and Asia. Sri Lanka's *Mahaweli Community Radio* (chapter 13) is one example of such a project. Other projects have been more political and have attempted to support the organizational and cultural initiatives of marginalized communities. These are the projects that tend to involve listeners in a participatory process. Haiti's *Radio Soleil* (chapter 9) and *Zoom Black Magic Liberation Radio* in the United States (chapter 10) are two examples.

Following the tradition of participatory communication, most of the chapters in this book are not written by impartial observers but by people with first-hand knowledge of community radio and with direct experience in the projects they write about.

The chapters are grouped into five sections, each concerned with one of the book's major themes: community, conflict, development, culture and beginnings. A brief passage at the beginning of each section introduces the theme.

COMMUNITY RADIO IN THE WORLD

Any examination of community radio must take into account the social and political environment in which it operates. This is particularly important when comparing and contrasting models from various regions. The following pages provide an overview of community radio experiences in various parts of the world and point to some of the current debates and concerns in each region.

Africa

Radio is undoubtedly the most important medium in Africa. Illiteracy and distribution problems mean that newspapers are unavailable to the vast majority of the population. Similarly, television is beyond the financial means of most people and national television service often does not extend to rural areas where much of the population lives.

Radio, on the other hand, is available almost everywhere. Receivers are relatively inexpensive and programming is inexpensive to produce and distribute. In virtually all African countries national radio services broadcasting from the capital and other major centres are the most important source of information.

While autonomous and participatory community radio does not exist in most African countries, *rural radio* does. Many countries have set up networks of rural radio stations that broadcast a mix of nationally and locally produced programmes.

Although rural radio stations share certain characteristics with community radio, they are usually managed from the capital by their national broadcasting systems through a department or production centre specifically concerned with rural radio. This lack of autonomy often results in programming that ultimately reflects the perspective of the central government rather than the local population. A second problem is that the rural stations often inherit the administrative and financial problems of the institutions that direct them.

Traditionally, rural radio in Africa tends not to involve the population in either decision-making or production. Programme content is usually determined by the government or by professionals in the stations, and almost never by the expressed concerns of the audience.

In the past two years a number of African countries have seen some remarkable political changes. These changes have been accompanied by a certain opening up of communication policies and as a result, a number of community radio experiments are taking form. In chapter 14, *Pluralist Responses for Africa*, Eugénie Aw discusses the significance of these changes and demonstrates how some communities have already been able to take advantage of the new openings. Pascal Berqué takes a closer look at one of these new experiments in chapter 12, *The Hard Lesson of Autonomy,* about a rural station in Mali.

The dramatic political changes taking place in South Africa are also being accompanied by fundamental changes in radio. For fifteen years the only challenge to the monopoly of the State-owned South African Broadcasting Corporation was the African National Congress' *Radio Freedom,* broadcasting on shortwave from neighbouring countries. Now, a large and dynamic community radio movement is preparing to go on the air before the end of 1992. In chapter 22, *When there is no Radio,* Edric Gorfinkel outlines the development of an organization that started with a "talking newspaper" project and will end with nothing less than a community radio station.

Asia

As with Africa, the broadcasting system in Asia was greatly influenced by the centralized, State-controlled traditions left behind by foreign colonizers. Designed as a means of propagating government thought, Asian broadcasting has never developed mechanisms to accept feedback or to provide the population with a means of articulating their aspirations and frustrations.

A second characteristic that Africa and Asia have in common is the importance of radio. Indeed, the central position of radio is a factor throughout the Third World. A worldwide survey conducted by UNESCO in 1986 indicated that there was an average of 160 radio receivers per thousand inhabitants in the developing countries. In contrast, there were only 39 television receivers per thousand inhabitants. These figures compare with 472 television receivers and 988 radio receivers per thousand inhabitants in the so-called developed countries.[1]

For the most part, Asia's broadcasting systems have been slower to shed their colonial past than have Africa's. However, some tentative steps have been taken and participants at a regional seminar on community radio held in Malaysia in 1990 described radio as being "in a state of ferment."

Sri Lanka's *Mahaweli Community Radio* project, discussed in chapter 13, has contributed to this "state of ferment" and to a growing understanding of the possibilities for local and national radio. *Mahaweli Community Radio* is operated as a branch of the national broadcasting system rather than as an autonomous community radio project, but it is an important step forward and the model has been adapted for use in a number of Asian countries.

In 1991 Vietnam undertook an important initiative with the establishment of a number of local community radio stations. The stations are operated by community representatives and enjoy a fairly high degree of local autonomy.

The Philippines stands out as an exception among Asian countries because its broadcasting system was heavily influenced by the commercial tradition of the United States. In addition to the private sector and a State radio network, there have been a number of rural radio projects established by universities and other institutions.

The lack of autonomous community radio stations in the Philippines has been partially compensated for by the ability of production groups to get airtime on commercial or public stations. *Radyo Womanwatch* (chapter 21) tells the story of one of these programmes.

Broadcasting remains a State monopoly in most Asian countries and the next few years will show us whether national broadcast organizations will be willing to share the airwaves with community groups and whether local stations will enjoy real autonomy in their organization and their programming.

Australia

While Australia is not represented in the book, it does have an active community radio movement with over one hundred stations on-air and more than fifty groups waiting for licenses to be granted. The stations broadcast in virtually all parts of the country, from large cities to tiny isolated "outback" communities.

Some of these stations (mainly in large cities) are licensed to provide a special broadcasting service, such as ethnic or Aboriginal programmes, or classical music, or educational programmes. The majority of them, however, are licensed to provide a broad-based community service and have a particular requirement to serve those groups in their community not served by national or commercial radio services; indigenous and ethnic minorities, women, the aged and unemployed youth are among the groups that have access to community radio.

Australia's community broadcasters derive their funding from three main sources: direct community support in the form of membership, subscriptions and donations (40%); "sponsorship," a highly restricted form of advertising (30%); and a variety of grants from federal, state and local government programmes.

Europe

The model of a centralized State-owned broadcast system that Europe exported to the detriment of its former colonies did not serve Europeans any better than it did Africans or Asians. The State monopolies lasted until the 1970s when the *free radio* movement swept through western Europe. At the height of this movement there were thousands of unlicensed pirate stations rebelling against the State's domination of the airwaves.

Only a handful of free radio stations survived into the mid-1980s. The ironic victim of its own success, the free radio movement withered when government monopolies broke apart and high-powered commercial radio networks pushed the free radios aside. Those that did survive were almost always in countries in which the State steadfastly refused to give up its monopoly. Amsterdam's *Radio 100* (chapter 2) is an exception and the station continues to broadcast as a pirate, even though Holland has a strong community radio movement.

Along with the decline of the free pirate stations came a demand for community radio, and almost all western European countries now have some form of legal community broadcasting. However, there are dramatic differences in form from one country to the next, and indeed, from one station to the next. *Radio Gazelle* (chapter 17) in France is one example.

In the eastern part of the continent, the situation varies dramatically from country to country and the broadcast environment seems to change on an almost daily basis. The clandestine *Radio Solidarnosc* had a brief moment of glory when Solidarity was still a banned trade union in Poland, but once walls and governments started falling the most visible trend was towards large-scale commercial radio, often fully or partially-owned by the giant media corporations of western Europe.

Despite the traditions of State monopoly and the strong presence of foreign capital — or perhaps because of them — there is a strong interest in alternative models of radio. Two examples are presented in this book, *Radio One* in Czechoslovakia (chapter 20) offers a cultural alternative for Prague's youth and *Echo of Moscow* (chapter 8) offers a political alternative in Russia.

Latin America

It was arguably in Latin America that the first community radio experiences were initiated almost fifty years ago. For years, State, private commercial, church, university, trade union and indigenous peoples' radio stations have combined to make the region's radio the most dynamic and diverse in the world.

In the past decade there has been an increase in the use of radio by popular groups. Some of these groups, such as Peru's Feminist Radio Collective (chapter 11), produce programmes and have them broadcast on the airwaves of commercial stations. Others use "bocinas," simple loud-speakers installed in shanty-towns, over which the community is able to have the voice the other media deny them. Thousands of tiny radio stations have sprung up in Argentina, so small they fall through the cracks of telecommunications legislation (chapter 19).

Other projects have emerged that define themselves as "educational" but that are not concerned with formal education. They have abandoned the classical methods of radio schools in favour of the tremendous educational possibilities of popular participation. Haiti's *Radio Soleil* followed this path for many years (chapter 9) and *Radio Asé Pléré An Nou Lité* in Martinique also continues to do so.

Native people have their own radio stations throughout the region. These stations broadcast in indigenous languages and are important place for cultural and political intervention. Chapter 15, *New Voices*, offers a look at how the structures of these stations in Mexico take into account the wide variety of local traditions and conditions that exist among native peoples.

Clandestine guerrilla stations have been instrumental in national liberation movements in many countries. *Radio Venceremos*, in El Salvador, broadcast the struggle of the Salvadorean people for eleven years before becoming legalized with the signing of a peace accord between the Farabundo Martí National Liberation Front and the government in February 1992 (chapter 7).

Hundreds of other examples exist: trade union-owned stations in Bolivia, stations run by peasant organizations in Ecuador, a women's station in Chile, over three hundred popular radio stations run by the Catholic Church and a handful of stations in Nicaragua courageously trying to survive in the hostile environment of that country.

North America

Community radio began quietly enough in North America when, in 1949, a California pacifist obtained a license for an FM station at a time when most people did not have FM receivers. Known as KPFA, the station is now listened to by hundreds of thousands of people in the San Francisco area and has an operating budget of US$1 million (chapter 5).

KPFA is not typical of the North American community radio experience. North America has almost as many different types of community radio as Latin America and it is hard to imagine that any of the 300 stations in Canada and the United States could be considered "typical." There are, however, a few generalizations that can be made. For example, *urban* community radio stations in North America tend to be more culturally and/or politically engaged and serve communities that are outside the "mainstream" because of their language, race, cultural interests, or politics. Vancouver's Co-op Radio is an example of this (chapter 18). In contrast, *rural* stations tend to be more in tune with the majority of their community, although the majority of a remote community often has little in common with the "mainstream" images and debates presented by urban-based radio networks.

In the remote regions of Canada's north, more than one hundred Native communities, some with only a handful of residents, have stations that fill the role of telephone, post office, meeting hall, and teacher. Broadcasting in their own languages, the volunteer programmers provide entertainment and essential information to people who may be cut off from the rest of the world for weeks at a time during winter storms. Given the important service these stations provide to Native people, they are drastically underfunded with annual budgets of around US$10,000. The stations of the *Wawatay Radio Network* described in chapter 3 are typical of these stations.

In the province of Quebec, site of AMARC's head office and of the first AMARC conference in 1983, there are 45 Native and 23 non-Native community radio stations. The non-Native stations tend to be further south than the native stations and serve larger populations, but even here we cannot find a "typical" station. Examples range from Montreal's *Radio Centre-Ville,* (chapter 6) which broadcasts in seven languages to an inner-city, mostly immigrant population, to *CFIM,* which broadcasts in French to a small population spread across the Magdalen Islands in the Gulf of St. Lawrence.

Pirate radio, a small but persistent phenomenon in North American broadcasting, is experiencing a resurgence as Black and anti-poverty groups challenge the system and set up low-powered neighbourhood stations (chapter 10).

As a result of deregulation in both Canada and the United States, commercial broadcasters are free to operate with fewer restrictions. They are carrying less news and information programming, engaging in fewer local productions and concentrating on the bland music formats that seem guaranteed to attract advertisers. In Canada, the State-owned CBC, traditionally the main source of quality programming, is suffering from budget cuts. For community radio in North America, the challenge continues to be to provide a service to those sectors of the population with cultural and political interests that are ignored by commercial or public radio.

Community radio broadcasters are working to make the airwaves accessible and open, and to transform radio into a medium in the service of their communities. With radio activists from around the world as your guides, this book offers a voyage to the heart of the alternative airwaves, and an understanding of why these activists have a passion for radio.

* * *

NOTES

1. UNESCO, 1989 pp 149, 156.

PART I: COMMUNITY

The defining characteristic of a community radio station is the participatory nature of the relationship between it and the community.

Most radio stations, community or otherwise, participate in some way in the lives of their listeners — announcing their news and events, presenting their music and reflecting their culture. However, few conventional stations offer their listeners a chance to participate by requesting a particular song, or to express an opinion on a topic defined by the radio station during phone-in shows.

Community radio, on the other hand, aims not only to participate in the life of the community, but also to allow the community to participate in the life of the station. This participation can take place at the level of ownership, programming, management, direction and financing.

Each of the radio stations looked at in this section has developed a particular way to enable and encourage community participation in one or more of these levels.

2

Radioproeflokaal Marconi

François Laureys

In Amsterdam, one can find more than 5,000 bars and cafés, from dark-brown to high-light, from cosy neighbourhood pubs to high-brow society-clubs, from no-future dumps to futuristic techno-spaces, and from gay-bars to dreary night-clubs. But there is no place quite like Radioproeflokaal Marconi: the Marconi Radio Tasters Café. As its name suggests, Marconi is more than a café, it's the heart of free radio in the Dutch capital.

Radioproeflokaal Marconi is located in an old school on a small canal just a little outside the city-centre and just down the street from Radio 100, an unlicenced community radio station founded in 1980. In the earlier days, I used to come here almost daily to have a chat with some of the other people from Radio 100 or with the listeners who would gather there. But since I stepped over to the 'settled' media, and started to earn a living two years ago as a journalist for the provincial radio, my visits to Marconi have become less frequent. I hadn't been there for a long time, when on May 15, 1991, I heard news of a police raid. When I arrived at the place everything was already over. "We knew this had to happen sometime. It's been seven years since the authorities last raided us," says an old radio acquaintance. "But look at the mess they made. We didn't expect them to come down on us that hard."

The place looks a mess indeed: glass is scattered all over the floor; the walls that used to separate the café and the studio have been demolished. Someone hands me a flyer, Radio 100's first official reaction to the raid. It reads:

> It is six in the evening. The strong arm is itching to hack out the rotten places in society. The troops advance on the Bilder-

> dijkstraat (the street where the broadcast studio of Radio 100 is housed) and environs. As is usual at this time on Wednesday evenings, Amsterdam's theatrical life is being discussed on Radio 100. The program *Playrol* is coming to a close when the doorbell rings...must be the blues show! The unsuspecting theatre woman who opens the door is trampled by a horde of defenders of the public order — in full regalia. The security dogfaces storm the illegal radio den. Soldiers' boots echo through the hall of the building, in search of suspicious conspirators. Meanwhile, the Marconi Radio Tasters Café is taken in hand by vermin with ears only for the orders of their superiors...The protesting café customers are hustled outside and the blue brotherhood begins to rearrange the building, in a search for criminal networks. Appointment books, shopping lists, computer files and phonographs are welcome booty. The roundup begins. Elsewhere in the city six people are hauled from their dinner tables, accused of being leaders of the radio-conspiracy, and thrown into the clink. Everything capable of producing sound disappears into mouldy sheds. Under the fedoras of the Secret Service, sardonic grins appear.

The studio equipment, the transmitter and the antenna have been confiscated, several people arrested, the radio café thoroughly demolished. Strangely enough, nobody seems defeated or depressed. A feeling of anger predominates. Rob, a volunteer programmer at the station, comments:

> We'll get over it. Just wait and see — with the help of our listeners and a few benefit events we'll be back within three weeks. What really bothers me is the fact that they arrested so many people. We don't have leaders. We're a grassroots organization which means that everybody who works with us has an equal voice in every decision concerning the radio. It looks like they want to have some scapegoats...or maybe they want to intimidate the 97 other programme-makers. I don't know. We'll have to see what their next step will be.

Two days later, Rob is arrested. His presentiment was right. This time, the authorities seem determined to finish this pirate radio business.

Radio 100 has been broadcasting on the FM band illegally at least since 1980, and hasn't had too much trouble with the authorities. Once in a while, the police would show up and confiscate the transmitter. But that's part of the game...With a little extra effort, a new transmitter would be obtained within a few days, and broadcasting would start again. This time the warning seems clear enough: as far as "they" are concerned, the game is over.

During the first weeks after the raid it becomes evident that the authorities did indeed spend a lot of time planning how to deal effectively with Radio 100 this time. During a six month period prior to the raid, a large team of undercover agents have been busy following programmers, tapping their phones, and listening to their broadcasts. Radioproeflokaal Marconi has been watched constantly. The postbox of Radio 100 has been emptied and the mail read. The bank accounts of both Marconi and Radio 100 have been studied and a list of regular contributors has been made up. In other words, an investigation that would make any member of the Mob flush with jealousy. The raid itself involved a police force of 150 men and four officers with another 150 guardians of the peace held back, just in case.

A criminal investigation it was, so a criminal organization it must be. The radio programmers who were arrested during and after the raid were charged with "membership in an organization whose intention it is to commit crimes." But where's the crime? Dutch law states that illegal broadcasting is a misdemeanour. In most cases a fine will settle the case. The police argued that "this bunch of anarchists grew to be a highly developed organization." Anarchists? Organization?

After ten days the charges are dropped. The jailed programmers are released.

In the meantime, several huge benefit parties have been organized all over Amsterdam. More than 2,000 people show up. Left wing parties on the local, national and European levels protest the raid. Hundreds of listeners support the station with financial donations. A Radio 100 flyer puts it this way:

> This deafening silence begs for a new sound. The call for social liberation of the airwaves echoes through the local cosmos. They can't do this! The listeners, too, keep dazedly twisting the frequency dials, in the throes of cold turkey. But

> the people and children of Radio 100 are feverishly resuming their public obsession. Waves of energy ripple through the city. Bicycle wagons full of discarded CD players arrive. The bank account of the radio climbs further into the black by the minute. Everyone joins in. The programmers are back at work.

And indeed, four weeks after the raid Radio 100 starts broadcasting again. As if nothing had ever happened.

THE VOICE OF THE SQUATTERS' MOVEMENT

Radio 100 is a bit of an anachronism. Between 1979 and 1985 there were dozens of FM pirates operating in Amsterdam. Most of them were commercially motivated: easy music and a lot of advertising. After 1983 the authorities started to pay attention to these illegal stations and most of them were closed down within a year. By 1985 Radio 100 was the only one left. Some former pirates were able to obtain licences to broadcast under conditions set by the government, but Radio 100 turned down offers of a licence. Claiming the right to freedom of expression they refused to submit themselves to the rules that would accompany legalization. Nowadays, Radio 100 is the only pirate station in Amsterdam with regular daily broadcasts.

The station's roots lay in the roaring year of 1980, when the squatters' movement in Amsterdam started to organize and rebel against evictions from squatted houses. Housing shortages (a product of speculation) and unemployment drove thousands of young people to squat in order to provide themselves with a home. This resulted in numerous violent clashes between the police and the squatters. In those days the radio station operated as an 'action-medium'. It was the voice of the squatters' movement, attacking the housing policies of the local government and mobilizing the militant segments of the city's population. During riots it would provide information about police movements and tell demonstrators how to avoid roadblocks and arrests.

In the following years, when the situation calmed down, partly due to the city's efforts to legalize squatted houses, the tone of the radio mellowed too. It started to focus more on musical and cultural developments. Also, within the station, a re-interpretation of the medium's possibilities took place. Why should a small group of people have the power to operate this radio? How could we involve listeners in the programmes, or even in the actual production of programmes? How could we let listeners participate more than simply via the phone? This is where the concept of the radio café came in.

Ingrid, who worked with Radio 100 from 1982 until 1987 recalls:

> At the end of 1984 we came to a point where we asked ourselves what was the point of going on like we were used to? On the one hand, we didn't want to be legalized. On the other hand, we were the last pirate radio left and we knew that in order to survive we had to gain the sympathy and the support of a broad audience. You know, the classic dilemma: because we were illegal we had to operate more or less 'underground', which made it difficult to make 'real' contacts with listeners or social and cultural organizations outside the squatters' movement. So we came up with this idea of a radio café — a place in the neighbourhood of our broadcasting studio. Here, people would be able to meet us without the stigma of illegality. The radio café would be what you might call 'the open door to our (illegal) radio'. We were determined to make our radio 'visual', to get out of the harness of having to be anonymous. 'Open radio' was our credo at that time. Getting other people, listeners, to participate in the radio. We were fed up with hiding ourselves. We wanted the radio to become a part of daily life for as many people as possible!
>
> So eventually we found this old school near our studio. The squatters there agreed with our proposal to turn two huge classrooms on the ground floor into a radio café, so we started building! We didn't have any money, but we got most of the things we needed from listeners and supporters. What we did was build a kind of big glass wall between the two rooms, dividing it into a bar side and a studio side. The idea was that people actually would be able to 'see' radio being broadcast. After two months of blood, sweat and tears we officially opened 'our Marconi' with a kind of press conference during which we also 'revealed' the location of our broadcasting antenna to the press.

I remember that. Searching my archives I find the press statement dated June 9, 1985:

> As far as we are concerned, we are fed up with this illegality that is imposed on us, as well as the anonymity that is connected with it. We demand the right to free communication! For our part, we will start to act as an open radio from now on. Everybody can and should know what we stand for. What does open radio mean to us?
>
> - the possibility of active participation by every listener.
> - a public room, accessible to anyone, with studio facilities: the radio café.
> - the possibility for people, groups and organizations to express and profile themselves on the air.
> - no hierarchical structures within the station. Every member has an equal say on all the matters which concern the radio. General meetings are public.
>
> ...We demand a frequency on which we can broadcast unhindered. If this demand is not complied with, we'll start broadcasting anyway.

A pretty heavy statement coming from just another pirate radio station...

> Ingrid:
>
> Not an ordinary pirate radio. We were a free radio: non-commercial, democratic, progressive...You know, we really felt like we had right on our side. All we asked for was a frequency! We didn't want to become a professional or a commercial station! Just a station for and with its listeners. We wanted to gain a large audience from different communities in town. We wanted to create this kind of creative melting pot, with the radio as the gentle fire under it. But we didn't want to beg for permission. If it couldn't be done legally, well sorry, we would just carry on illegally.

As a matter of fact, Radio 100 did succeed in becoming this strange melting pot of different groups and cultures. Listening to its programmes, you might find an Indian programme followed by an hour of punk music, a two hour African music show and a theatre programme. And they've stuck to this idea. A flyer issued after the 1991 raid reads:

> We exist now more than ever. We are not criminals but the criminal organization of dissatisfaction. The infiltrators of the eardrums, the foam on the airwaves. We rule nothing out and broadcast it all. We never dial the right number but always get through. We continue fighting the air war, the other offensive has begun. We have joined in conspiracy with palace revolutionaries, Blackfoot Indians, kiosk runners, barkeepers, tax-evaders, crown prince Willem Alexander, black riders, cyberpunks, house-wives, narco-traffickers, superheroes, computer pioneers, jugglers, deserters, political tourists and other brilliant dilettantes. If they're looking for trouble, keep listening. Radio 100 is far beyond 1992 in ideas and technique. The terrible echoes of our silence will ring out everywhere.

That is Radio 100 indeed. I don't think the term "community radio" really covers this kind of radio. The kind of people it attracts would probably better fit under something like "a movement": sometimes very tangible (like the squatters' movement used to be), and other times more diffuse, less perceptible, but still there somewhere under the surface of city life. "Free radio" fits quite well — the station drifts on the input of its programmers and listeners, independent of commercial or political powers, free from pressures on programming, altogether free of mind and choice. As such, Radio 100 is one of the pivots on which subcultural Amsterdam hinges.

But when the radio café was opened, Ingrid had in mind that the radio had to break out of this subculture and open itself to a broader audience:

> Me and some other people felt the atmosphere within this 'scene' was suffocating, we reflected too little on things that happened outside our 'subcultural' perception. I felt that to really achieve some changes within the radio, we had to broaden our view. This is what I thought a radio café could bring about. But I think we never really managed to break out. In the beginning, we tried to create an 'objective' atmosphere in Marconi, to attract 'ordinary people', and not only activists, squatters and punks. But it soon appeared that Marconi especially attracted marginals; maybe this was due to the fact that our prices were very low...Sometimes it really looked like a kind of human zoo. You

> would have some alcoholic bums, spaced-out weirdos, a couple of tourists and a few programmers hanging around. Not always a very stimulating crowd, though it could be fun sometimes. Later it became clear to me that a lot of people didn't want it to be different. They felt Marconi should be a place for our kind of people. Well, to achieve that is not too difficult, you know. You just play loud punk-music all the time, and you can be sure of a select company! In my eyes, the experiment failed, though it might still provide a good function for a select group of people...

Somewhat disappointed, Ingrid left the radio in 1987 and started working as a journalist for (legal) local and regional radio.

Rob started to work with Radio 100 at approximately the same time as Ingrid left. He disagrees with her view on the development of the radio café:

> I think Marconi grew to be one of the meeting-places of alternative Amsterdam. Look around at who's sitting here: those guys over there are Moroccan. They come and drink tea here almost every day. That group over there is from Radio Scorpio in Belgium, paying us a visit. You know the people at the bar, programme-makers. There are some people who live here. Sitting outside in the sun the usual bunch of acrobats and clowns who train in the old gym-room of the school. Quite an international public, eh? Apart from that, I think Marconi is important for the radio because it is the only place where programmers can meet. Our broadcasting studio is in another building, where we don't have extra space. Happily, it's just around the corner, so most programme-makers come here before or after their programme, to chat a while or have a laugh. Marconi is also the place where we have our general meetings — every Tuesday evening. Everybody from the radio can come, but it's not obligatory. Most of the time approximately twenty out of the one hundred collaborators show up. In extraordinary situations, like after the police raid, everybody comes to the meetings. That can be quite a spectacle! But at 'normal' meetings we discuss the current affairs of the radio, the technical problems, the financial situation, the programming, and so on. We also make plans for the near future. That can vary from organizing a benefit party to preparing a live broadcast from somewhere else in town or making plans for cooperation with video and computer groups. We get pretty

wild ideas sometimes! During that meeting people can also come by if they have new programme ideas and want to get some air time on the radio. Generally, if the ideas or concepts are original, they'll be granted one month of probation-time and can more or less start right away!

Last but not least, Marconi is a source of income for the radio. It doesn't make a huge profit, but that is due to the fact that the prices are very low and that it is run by volunteers...Some of them forget to charge their customers, others make mistakes when counting the change or serve too large portions, and sometimes money just 'vanishes'. But we still manage to save some money for the radio! You know, when I heard about the raid at the radio and at Marconi, I first thought this would be the end of it. Now, I think the raid has given us a new impulse. We tended to work too much on automatic pilot lately. Now that we have seen, once more, how many people are willing to back us in hard times, how much energy we can develop in a short time and how many people we were able to mobilize, I think we're in for the next decade!

* * *

3

To Tell the People — Wawatay Radio Network

Lavinia Mohr

Fifteen hundred kilometres northwest of Toronto, Canada's largest city, sits the Cree village of Sandy Lake in the boreal forest. The settlement is one of about 30 with a community radio station linked to the Wawatay Radio Network (WRN).

For five weeks in the winter an ice road stretches into the white distance from Ghost Point on the shore of Sandy Lake. Trucks carrying gasoline and building supplies from the south ply the road carved over dozens of frozen lakes dotting the Canadian Shield. When the road melts, the village will once again be accessible only by air, the same as all but a handful of the more than 40 villages that make up the Nishnawbe Aski Nation. The ice road season is the time for much visiting between relatives from different villages who don't see each other throughout the remainder of the year.

The villages of the Nishnawbe Aski Nation are spread throughout an area about the size of France. It is the ancestral home of about 20,000 Oji-Cree and Cree-speaking Indian people. Some have maintained the traditional hunting and fishing way of life. Many more, through years of paternalistic government policies, have become dependent on handouts. Millions of government dollars are spent on welfare payments, and almost none for native economic development in this remote area.

Sandy Lake's fifteen hundred inhabitants make it one of the larger settlements. In the summer, Ghost Point's rough hewn log stage sets the scene for Treaty Days. Government Indian Affairs agents come every year (formerly by ten day canoe voyage, now by air) to honour their treaty obligation to hand out 5 dollars to every living soul at a feast held for the occasion. They have been coming since 1910, the year the Sucker clan gave up 31,000 square kilometers of land for an initial payment of $970, with a promise that the King "for as long as the rivers run" would provide flour, bacon, tea, shot, powder, fishing gear and a school on a reserve that eventually took the form of 44 square kilometers on the lake shore.

The first representatives of the Canadian government appeared in Sucker clan lands in 1909. Police officers came to take away their leader, He Who Stands in the Southern Sky, also known as Jack Fiddler. Fiddler was charged with murder for exercising the chief's duty to end the agony of the pain-ridden incurably ill when all else had failed. Far away from the forest, in a Royal North West Mounted Police jail, Jack Fiddler, the old chief of a people who had never relinquished sovereignty of their ancestral land, slipped away from his guard and killed himself rather than submit to white man's justice. His brother, taken with him, died later of tuberculosis in Stony Mountain Penitentiary three days before a federal government pardon order reached the prison. Back in the forest, Jack Fiddler's bewildered people soon gave up their land to the agents of the "Great White Father."

Sixty years later, Jack Fiddler's grandson, Chief Thomas Fiddler, founded Wawatay Native Communications Society, based in the small town of Sioux Lookout. Another of his clansmen, James Fiddler, founded the community radio station in Sandy Lake before he died of tuberculosis at the age of 28.

The James Fiddler Memorial Radio Station occupies a rough one story wooden building just up the road from the Sandy Lake nursing station. In front, a pile of firewood waits to be taken in to the large wood stove that heats the building's seven rooms. Like nearly all the buildings in Sandy Lake, with the exception of the nursing station and the school, there is no running water. Outside, at the back, a satellite dish silently watches the sky, receiving the TV Ontario signal that also carries Wawatay Radio Network from Sioux Lookout hundreds of kilometers to the south. Off to one side stands the small Canadian Broadcasting Corporation (CBC) transmitter tower that broadcasts the national English radio service as well as the community radio signal. At 100 watts, the transmitter more than covers the reserve. By agreement, the CBC signal is cut and replaced by the local station at certain times of the day. As with the other community radio stations in the Nishnawbe Aski territory, the language of the radio is aboriginal Cree or Oji-Cree. These are the tongues of daily life for most people.

A few hours by airplane to the south, in the town of Sioux Lookout, Wawatay Native Communications Society's dozens of employees work in the Thomas Fiddler Memorial Building. The office and studio building is named in honour of their founder, Sandy Lake's old chief. Wawatay serves the Nishnawbe Aski Nation territory with a television network, a trail radio system for hunters on the trapline, a telephone operator translation service and a newspaper, in addition to the Wawatay Radio Network (WRN) carried on the community radio stations. Of all these communication services, the local community radio stations linked by the network are closest to the daily lives of the people. Nothing important happens in the communities without being channeled through their radio.

Wawatay got its start when the northern chiefs decided that something needed to be done about modern communications in their territory. Mike Hunter, a long time Wawatay Board member from Peawanuck who works in Polar Bear Park on the west coast of Hudson Bay, explains:

> I believe it was 1972. I was a Band Councillor then. There was a big meeting of the chiefs in Big Trout Lake. There was no communications of any kind in those days at all, period. The only thing Bell Telephone had in those days was the HF radio system. That's high frequency radio telephone communication system. And it was inadequate.

In most reserves, the only HF radio belonged to the private Hudson's Bay Company store. To get a message to a neighbouring reserve, a chief had to use the store's radio to send word south where it travelled as a telegram over an 1,100 mile route back north again.

> So all the chiefs said, 'Let's have our own communication system. If we can get a license, we can have an HF radio communication system on our own frequency and we can communicate ourselves'. And that's when it started.

The Canadian government provided funding for an experimental project to establish an HF radio network between the reserves, and Wawatay Native Communications Society was formed to take over the operation of the network.

Wawatay Radio Network producer Bill Morris tells how Wawatay got its name:

> The one who named Wawatay was Mason Koostachin from Fort Severn. 'So everybody, what are we going to call this society?' Nobody volunteered. He said, 'Let's call it Wawatay.' Oh, that was nice. That word means northern lights. We look up in the clear skies of the northern part of Ontario every night. The whole sky will be covered with northern lights. And that's what wawatay means.

In its very early days, Wawatay started the publication of a newspaper. Following that, it turned its attention to the provision of a trail radio system which used portable high frequency radios. Wawatay owns and maintains a large number of these radios which are rented out during the season to trappers who are out on their traplines for extended periods of time. Trappers and their families use them to communicate with the base HF radios in the settlements and with other trappers. They are used in normal times to keep in touch with relatives and friends, to share the events of daily life and to share information about the weather and the movements of migratory animals. But the primary purpose of the trail radio system is for emergency use. It has been credited with saving many lives.

Soon after setting up the trail radio system, Wawatay set to work on community radio. The way had been paved by an experimental station set up in 1973 in Big Trout Lake, the largest community in the territory, with the help of government funding. As soon as other villages heard about it, they wanted a community radio station of their own. The idea of community radio immediately found immense popularity. Garnet Angeconeb explains:

> CFTL in Big Trout Lake was the first community radio station ever in the Nishnawbe-Aski area. It took off. People really grasped on to the idea of how powerful community radio could be in a setting where communications are limited.
>
> At that time when there weren't any telephones in the community in people's homes, it acted as a communication tool within the village. People passed messages on. The community's leaders could use the airwaves to talk to people about concerns or issues. People were able to hear at once what was happening. It created dialogue within the community.

Since that time, the villages have acquired modern telephones as well as very limited television service. But the community radios established throughout the territory have maintained their vital role at the centre of community life.

In the nineteen seventies, the publicly owned Canadian Broadcasting Corporation (CBC) implemented a plan to provide its national radio service to all communities in Canada with 500 or more people. The experiment in Big Trout Lake had shown that there was a great popular demand for locally-originated radio in northern Ontario. The CBC agreed to allow community access to its repeater transmitters during certain hours each day. Very simple radio studios were installed for that purpose. However, there were only a few villages in Nishnawbe Aski territory that benefited. Sandy Lake was one of the few.

Most villages were too small to qualify for a CBC repeater and the community access radio station that it made possible. They had to start up community radios on their own with the help of Wawatay.

In spite of being one of the newest and smallest settlements, Muskrat Dam was the first village in the territory to start a community radio station independent of the CBC repeater/community access station system like the one set up in Sandy Lake. Wawatay Radio Network producer Bill Morris has family in Muskrat Dam, a community of about 200 established in 1966 on the site of a fishing camp. They wanted to maintain a more traditional way of life than in the village they came from. Bill helped his grandfather build cabins during summer breaks away from high school in a southern city.

Bill recalls what it was like at the station when he was the manager there, before becoming a network producer.

> The Band Council came to see me and they asked me, 'Okay, would you be able to work at the radio?' And I said, 'Well, you know, if my health is good, sure, I could work or volunteer. I'll do my best'.
>
> Well, I started working. There's no hydro (electricity) over there. Well, there's hydro, but you can't use the heaters. Cause all there is, is just a diesel (generator). It's only good for lights. How we heat the building is use wood stoves. There was really help doing it, especially in the winter time. I was going and get the wood. And they were going and chop the wood and heating up the whole building. They don't get paid for it. They do it volunteer.
>
> And how did they get my money? They just had to do some fund raising. Like play bingo (on the radio). And make money off the

dedications. When somebody wants to send one song, okay, they pay twenty-five cents. But on bingo I used to make, well, okay, about thirty dollars one night, or sometimes fifty for a week.

So anyways, with that fifty dollars I could maintain my radio. Like, I could buy gas. Maybe five gallons of gas. It was five dollars... about four-fifty, five dollars a gallon of gas. You have to go and get the wood maybe five miles away from the community. So you use a skidoo. And a power saw too. So I need gas. I use that radio station money to buy gas to get wood. And also there's some calls I used to make. There's a telephone, a pay phone. Sometimes I phone up Wawatay or someplace.

In that time I knew some people from Winnipeg. I used to get the records from over in 'Peg, cause I knew some people. So I usually phone them up, 'Okay. Can you send me some records?' So, they send me, and I send 'em the money back.

I used to open my radio at about 6:30 in the morning, I guess. Well, actually, I'd go there 6:30 in the morning, or a little after six o'clock, especially in winter time, and start to heat up the building. And I'd go on air at seven o'clock in the morning. That's when the people want that. They want to open the radio from seven to nine. They want it opened early in the morning, because the kids are going to school. So I usually tell them, 'O.K., you guys. Kids should get ready. It's almost nine o'clock. It's really cold.' And at nine o'clock, shut the radio off. Then open the radio at 11 o'clock until one in the afternoon. I usually get the volunteers from twelve to one. I open again at four o'clock in the afternoon until about ten o'clock. I usually get volunteers in the evenings. Maybe I'll be going on there sometimes one hour or two hours in the evening.

The volunteers have their own records. Everybody buys his own records. They bring their own type of music they want, although we have records at the station. But they have their own records too. They bring them up and they play their own music, and also they come down here and they tell stories too. And also elders. They'd come over here and go on.

Or they take messages. Somebody will call from outside the community so they take messages there because there's a telephone there. So every time somebody calls from outside the community, and they says, 'Here's a message to a certain person...' You're supposed to call to Round Lake, maybe Bearskin Lake or Sachigo. Or to

Kasabonika or to Big Trout Lake. See, people calls in, especially in the evenings.

We have a Board of Directors and our directors, they're the ones who set the directions to me. We have about seven directors. And they're the ones who give the directions — what I have to do —and set up a schedule.

The kids... they come in on the four to five. And they play rock music. Mostly the kids are from nine years old, till fourteen. But I usually supervise with them and I teach them how to operate the radio. And then five to six, probably somebody'll be coming on. Six to seven, I usually get somebody who has the trail radio at home — HF radios. That person, he talks to the other communities. And that's how we get news from outside our community. That person who has the HF radio will be based at home. He comes on at six o'clock and tells, 'Okay. This is what they said over in the other place...' So that's how we get the stories from outside the community. This is the time before Wawatay Radio Network was in, see.

In the night time I used to listen to the Winnipeg (English language) station. What I used to do, just before I go to the radio, I'd record the news. I knew what's going on. So, I knew who was playing hockey in Sioux. I record that and then I write it up (in Cree). Then I'd go on the radio, 'Okay. This is what's happening. This is what's happening in Winnipeg.'

Even the weather. I'd get the weather from Winnipeg. Because Winnipeg's not too far from Muskrat Dam. Well, actually, I don't know how far is it, but... Like if they have really a rough weather over there, we get that weather just in 24 hours. That's how long it travels. So I usually predict the weather too. I usually used to talk about Mr. Trudeau at that time, when he was the Prime Minister. And I say, 'Gee, it's cold here, and now Mr. Trudeau's way down in the south in the Caribbean Islands. He's on holidays. And there we are here. It's cold, you know.' They used to like it when I used to do that.

Wawatay in Sioux Lookout helped Muskrat Dam get the equipment for the radio station and sent a technician in to install it. The community raised the $2,000 to pay for it. Wawatay's search for the right equipment led them to a small hand made FM transmitter. Wawatay technician George Daigle picks up the story:

> It was designed by E.E. Stevens in Ottawa. He was an electronic engineer. He started building these little transmitters for FM radios. They were three quarters of a watt, which was plenty for a little community. It was just fantastic — FM Radio. It was perfect. He made the antenna out of copper tubing water pipes.
>
> Steven's been making these transmitters now for, I don't know, twelve years. He sends them all over. You'll probably see some down in South America. They're all over the place.
>
> They're unique. There's no tuning on them. You just turn it up until it starts to distort. Crank her back a little bit, and that's it. That's your tuning. That's all there is to it. It's got a three position switch for the meter. You can tell if your antenna's no good. It tells you if there's been damage. You can monitor the signal going into your transmitter. And the one going out, and the one reflected back. It tells you everything you need to know about the antenna. You just click, click, click everything works fine and that's it. That's all there is to your transmitter.

Wawatay ordered 25, and in 1977 went up to Muskrat Dam to install the first one in defiance of the CRTC, Canada's broadcasting regulatory agency. Former Wawatay Executive Director Garnet Angeconeb puts it this way:

> At first we had some problems dealing with government regulations and so on with using this transmitter in that it didn't meet government specifications. Therefore the CRTC wouldn't license these things. But we went ahead and used them anyway, simply because it was the right thing to do. I mean everything looked logical up north. There weren't any other frequencies to interrupt or to interfere with. So it was just right. We went ahead and used them anyway and in Muskrat Dam that transmitter proved to be really useful.

Eventually the CRTC relented and gave Wawatay licenses for all 25 transmitters. One by one, the communities of the north raised the money to purchase the equipment and Wawatay flew in a technician to install them. George Daigle tells how it's done:

> Jeez, it's cold waitin' for a wood stove to get warmed up. One community I went to, this was a while ago... it's about eight years ago, I

guess. They had no place for me to sleep — nowhere. They put me in this wood shack. I had to stay there overnight. It was in the fall. It was snowing a bit. That was quite a night, that one. They had a little wood stove in the corner, but you could see right through the walls. Snow would come in. I had to sleep on top of a pile of wood. Keep away from the ground, because it was snowing out. That was quite something. That's the roughest I've ever seen up there.

Sometimes you stay in a house that somebody has given to the Band. The Band built them a new house and moved them over there. So they just kept this one house for visitors. They have no running water. They got no lights. All they got is a bed and sometimes it's only a foam on top of a ply-wood. We never get blankets. You don't get bedding. You just get a bed. You bring your own sleeping bag. Most of them, there's no heat in there. They'll supply you with wood. They'll light the fire and they'll bring you water. They don't have restaurants there, so you got to bring all your grub.

I go in there, I want to stay a week. Because I don't know what's going to go wrong.

It takes a day to find your room, get organized, get people up there, find where the radio station's gonna be installed, bring the equipment there. It's hard to get around cause there's no vehicles. So you got to lug everything. It takes awhile to get around. So I usually chuck off the first day.

Next day, you install the radio station. It don't take so long. It doesn't take you long to hook up that kind of equipment. In about half a day — you're done.

The latest stations, we even put the transmitter up on the top of the TVO (TV Ontario) tower. They allowed us to put it on theirs. So all I really have to do is shimmy up the tower, stick a pipe in there, clamp the antenna on it and put a couple of clamps on the tower and come back down. And that's it! You just screw it into the transmitter. No tuning, no nothing. There it goes. On the air. It's as fast as that.

And then we train everybody...how everything works. How to shake it down. And they're on their own. Kenina (Kakekayash, the Wawatay Radio Network manager), usually she'll do the paper work for licenses.

And then I'll stay there for a couple of days. Go look at the HF radio, and do a little work on that, maybe. Fix up the antenna. Change the antenna. Just to stick around the community. Not go far. They'll come back about a day or two later and ask questions. Not the same day. I'd rather just stand back and watch. They won't ask any questions. Finally, when they know that we're about ready to leave, then everybody's there and asking questions. So I've learned my lesson. I stay there for a couple or three days, and eventually, when they get to run it more and more, then they start asking questions. 'How do you operate this, now?' And then you can start telling them.

And if they have problems, you're there, you know? After they start, there's always something that could go wrong, so you give it a few days, let them run into the problems.

Then you show them: 'You do this wrong, you do this right'. You go back then and get away from there, and listen again. I bring my own radio and listen to 'em at home. And, sure enough, it don't take 'em long. They're right in there, and away they go. Then they're fine. They're mobile. And then from there they grow.

If they didn't have a TVO tower, we go in the bush, cut a pole from a tree. You come in there and plant it. Dig a hole, nail the antenna on top of it, and then put up the pole. We always brought extra because if we drop that pole, so much for the antenna! I've done that a few times. I always bring two. Cause we have a bunch of antennas. We have 'em spare because lightening hits 'em and rips 'em apart.

This one community there, I remember, there must have been about, I don't know, fifty people around watching me working all this time. And as soon as I said, 'Well, okay, this is it, she's on the air!'...Zoom. Everybody disappeared. As soon as I said that the radio station was on the air. They were gone. It was really funny. They all went home to listen to their radios, I guess. They were already prepared. They had an FM radio. All the time that I worked there, installing the radio station, there was crowds watching from the window. They was watching from the windows everywhere. It was quite a feeling, to be bringing something that they never had before, something that they really wanted.

According to Garnet Angeconeb,

Community radio in an Indian community in the Nishnawbe Aski Nation is part of the overall infrastructure the same way as roads in a

> municipality in the south. Community radio is different in the isolated north as opposed to radio in southern communities. There is no other way of getting local information exchange within the community without the radio station. In the north it's the only radio station that people can tune into locally. Therefore, it becomes an intricate part of the community.

The James Fiddler Memorial Radio Station in Sandy Lake is an example. The station is under the direction of the Wendomowin (To Tell the People) Communications Society whose president is Abel Fiddler. He says that one of the most important things about the radio is "getting word to the people."

> We're really close in the community, eh? Not like white people. We really care about each other. Like if there is an emergency at the nursing station, a whole bunch of people go there. In case of emergency in the southern areas, they don't care. Here everybody goes.
>
> If somebody is lost in the bush, people carry portable radios with batteries. And like if anybody is found, and a whole bunch of people are in the bush [searching], they listen to the radio all the time and they know right away the person has been found and the searchers come back.

Menashi Meekis is a young man who took on the job of managing Sandy Lake's radio station, a difficult task because of the chronic shortage of money. He describes another way in which the station is integral to keeping the community in touch with itself.

> Most people are related here. If somebody dies, one of the band councillors calls me up and we have to go on the air and I come. Sometimes we stay open all night when someone dies. I have to get volunteers. Sometimes I have to show up at four or five [in the morning]. We play gospel music until everyone knows. If someone is watching TV, he goes to the radio and opens his radio. We have a pirate TV dish and they turn it off. If they see the picture go off, they would wonder and they turn the radio on. During the time the councillors would be driving around telling the relatives to open the radio and to tell them what happened. After everybody knows, then the Band

comes in and comes on the air to tell the people. That's why we have to open early so people can open their radios before the Sandy Lake Band comes on to tell them what happened. So we're pretty close.

The radio station is integral to the rhythm of daily life. Music lifts the spirits of all ages, each having their own time during the day. After school hours for the young, mid-morning for the elders, Sunday afternoon for the religious. All day long the music is punctuated by the all important phoned-in messages that are repeated several times, at the end of songs. An elderly widow calls to say that one of her grandsons should come to chop firewood for her. There is no gas for sale today at one place, but there is at the other. The plane from Sioux Lookout has arrived. Someone's cousins are driving in tonight on the ice road from Weagamow but he has to meet them half way at midnight with a can of gas because they don't have enough to make it. Jennifer's mother is looking for her. Would whoever took Bill's grey suitcase at the air strip please return it. The nursing station will have a visiting doctor today and the following people have appointments. The medicines for the health centre came up on the plane today and people waiting can pick them up now.

The school, the police, the drug and alcohol commission, the recreation clubs, the firehall, the women's baseball team, all the several churches each have their alloted regular hour. Sometimes they have serious matters to discuss, other times they just chat and play music to help everyone's day along while the important messages are phoned in and announced. Other hours are given to members of the community, sometimes in pairs, who like to come and play their favourite music for the general amusement of Sandy Lake.

And then there is the indispensible radio bingo every Thursday night. People come into the station throughout the day to buy their cards for the evening's game. Board members drive around during the day selling cards to people who can't get to the station. It's a major form of entertainment, and it raises most of the money for the station. The bingo master calls out the numbers over the radio, and the winner calls in when he or she has a bingo. The money raised pays the electricity, phone and gas bills and other costs. It also goes towards the occasional airplane ticket for the local hockey team to go to the Northern Tribes playoff in Sioux Lookout, or for a band member to go to a relative's funeral in another village.

The winners come down to the station to get their cash, and they often spend a good portion of it right then and there on Nevada tickets. Nevada tickets are like scratch and win lottery cards, except that they have to be torn open to see if you have a winner. You get your cash on the spot if you do. It's not unusual to see a group of men standing around the trash barrel near the front door of the station deftly flipping open a handful of Nevada tickets while they talk over the day's events. By Band Council order, the radio station has the monopoly of this popular way to try your luck. The proceeds help keep the station on the air.

The Wawatay Radio Network is heard a few hours a day in the Nishnawbe Aski Nation villages with a community radio station. The broadcasts are uplinked live from Wawatay's Sioux Lookout offices piggybacked with TV Ontario's satellite signal. Wawatay has been extremely adept over the years at dealing with southern institutions such as TV Ontario, the Ontario public educational television network. TV Ontario was setting up a satellite receiving dish in each village to get their service into the remote areas of northern Ontario. Wawatay succeeded in getting TV Ontario to squeeze its radio network signal onto the satellite and to set up a simple switching system to feed the signal into the community radio transmitters when Wawatay is broadcasting.

Kenina Kakekayash from the Round Lake reserve manages the radio network. She started with Wawatay as an interpreter for their telephone translation service. The service provides interpretation between northern callers and telephone company operators. Kenina was later given the responsibility of travelling from village to village to talk to the native leaders about the idea of setting up the radio network. She recalls the excitement of those times.

> We had to meet the band leaders, informing them, finding out what they thought about it and if they were going to support that thing. They did. Everybody was excited. They were so happy. 'It's about time that we're gonna put the network together. We're gonna hear the news.' I did a lot of travelling. At first it was really hard because of the technology words. You have to say them in our native language. As time went by, it became easier.

The network provided even more impetus for the villages that didn't have their own community radio station to get one set up. They couldn't be part of the network without a local station. Kenina worked with many communities helping them get on the air. But there are still communities without a station. Executive Director Lawrence Martin wants to see them all in the network. He thinks this will provide a new challenge for Wawatay: "It's gonna be interesting because they're more in the southern part. Their language is not as strong as the ones up here." However, Wawatay faced a serious setback to its plans to complete coverage of the territory, when the Canadian government made deep cuts to funding for native communications societies in 1990.

WRN broadcasts 95% of its daily programming in both languages spoken in the Nishnawbe Aski Nation, Cree and Oji-Cree. Several northern producers based in the communities put together stories that Sioux Lookout and Moose Factory network staff use in combination with their own material. Sioux Lookout produces the Oji-Cree programmes and Moose Factory on the western shore of Hudson Bay produces the Coastal Cree programmes. Programmes focus on international, national, and regional news, culture and traditions, children and youth, and important issues such as native self-government, the education system, and the extremely high suicide rate among the young. Weather, birthdays and sports (hockey is played with a passion in the north) are not forgotten.

Garnet Angeconeb believes that WRN helps the people of the Nishnawbe Aski Nation understand the forces of the outside world that affect them.

> I see an educational process happening here. You know, not only do they learn about Indian issues, but they also learn about the political process, whether it's provincial politics, whether it's federal politics. They begin to understand why things are the way they are. For example, Indian people, like anywhere else in the world, use energy. They use fuel. They use gasoline to run their machines, skidoos or outboard, what have you. And the way they get their gasoline in the north is it's flown in by aircraft. That's the only means of transporting fuel to most communities. And the cost of gasoline is extremely high in the north. And every time the prices go up, they just blame either the airlines or the local store. Of course the airlines and the local stores have to make their profit as well. But there are other factors as to why the price of gasoline goes up. The politics in Alberta could affect the prices of gasoline, for example. The politics in the Middle East can affect the prices of gasoline. And so what you begin to see then is that, hey, these things aren't just happening locally. They're

> happening in other parts of the country. And in other parts of the world. So what you begin to see is Indian people not only taking an interest in what is happening locally, or regionally, they're beginning to take an interest in what's happening nationally. And even beyond that, internationally.

Of the 53 aboriginal languages still spoken in Canada, only a few are considered by Canadian officials to have any chance of survival. Cree is one of the few. The native people of northern Ontario consider that their community radios are crucial to the survival of their language. Garnet Angeconeb explains.

> The guiding principle behind all the community radio movement is based on language. The success story had one focus and that is language and culture. The programming is in the language of the people. When people listen to the Wawatay Radio Network the elders are able to relate to what is happening as well as the young people. Hopefully through the radio network people are able to strengthen their language, their culture and their identity. And that's really important. Many people at Wawatay have always said that it is important for aboriginal people to try and keep their language. I'm a firm believer in that. If aboriginal people lose their language, they don't have any other place to go to regain it, or their culture for that matter. It's not like a person living in Canada who is of Italian background. They could always go back to their mother country to regain their language and their culture. But here in Canada, for the aboriginal people, this is the motherland of the culture, this is the homeland of the aboriginal languages, and if they're lost, they're lost and gone forever. There is no other place to go. So through Wawatay our argument has always been that we have to do everything possible to strengthen our languages and keep them alive.
>
> People are getting satellite dishes to beam in TV, and when you look at the television set in the living room in a northern community, the programming's really irrelevant. You see a little kid rhyming lines off a sitcom — Rambo movies. And the challenge to keep our language alive becomes real. It's not a fantasy. The most frustrating part of my job when I was Executive Director of Wawatay was trying to convince decision makers in places like Ottawa or Toronto that northern Ontario

has a unique lifestyle. The Indian communities are unique up there. They're very rich people. They may not be rich in terms of financial resources or anything like that, but they are rich in terms of their culture and their language. And we have to preserve that.

* * *

Note: The conversations upon which this story is based took place mainly in 1989. A year later, Canadian government financial contributions to the aboriginal communications organizations that provide a broadcast or printed voice for native people were drastically cut back in a move that seems designed to mute those voices. Twenty one such groups throughout Canada have cut staff, reduced operations or gone out of existence. Wawatay's ability to provide technical maintenance for the community radio stations and trail radios of Nishnawbe Aski is being severely tested, as is the network itself.

* * *

4

Lessons from a Little-Known Experience: Radio Candip

Eugénie Aw

While the struggle for democratization has proven difficult, profound changes are taking shape in the Central African country of Zaire. Without a doubt, one of the essential tasks within the framework of democratisation, will be popular access to communications — and in particular, radio.

Zaire has seen the emergence of a radio experience which puts the ideal of popular participation into practice. Known as Radio Candip, the project is integrated into a larger framework of development, social economics, and education — not an original concept for African rural radio. However, what sets Radio Candip apart from many such models is its reliance on the local population — radio by or with the people, rather than for the people.

DIALOGUE AND COMMUNICATION

If rural radio stations are to fulfil a role as a modern and supplementary aid to development, the various sectors of the population must be able to participate in the programming and have access to it. Passive listening must be transformed into dialogue and communication.

With this ideal in mind, Radio Candip was established in 1977, as a project of the Center for Radio Broadcasting and Educational Activities. The Center is part of the Bunia Higher Education Institute, located in northeastern Zaire, a heavily populated region in which one million people live off of agriculture and raising cattle.

Like many rural stations, Radio Candip broadcasts programmes with information intended to help increase production. It also emphasizes programming which responds to the questions and needs of its listeners, and encourages people to work together on community projects.

> The radio speaks to them in their language, informs them of their duties and rights, gives them advice on how to solve problems they face, and on activities they can develop with their families and in the village. (Pickery, 1987)

Radio Candip's production teams produce programming in seven languages and a variety of programme formats. One of the most interesting of these formats is found is the station's participatory programmes based on material supplied by radio clubs and mini-studios.

RADIO CLUBS

Soon after Radio Candip began broadcasting, the station's personnel promoted the setting up of *radio clubs* in villages throughout the region. A radio club is a group of people who come together to listen to the radio, discuss its programmes, and move on to action. The clubs often grow out of social or youth movements, are initiated by a dynamic leader, or more simply, by the example of a neighbouring village. They include a diverse presence of social groups, development organisations, and local authorities.

These groups prepare listener reports, audience testimony, and questions, and send them by mail to the station. By February 1987, there were 749 clubs for 6 language groups: Nandé, Lendu, Alur, Swahili, Lugbara, and Lingala.

> Villagers are encouraged to listen to the radio "with their ears, eyes, head and arms;" to understand the programmes; to look around them and compare the radio message to the realities lived; to understand why; to reflect upon their motives and behaviour; and to extend what they hear into concrete actions, solutions to the problems they face.

The radio clubs are also the focal point for audience feedback. They allow the listeners a channel for input into the activities and programming of the station: Are the programmes broadcast responding to the needs of the people? What are their problems and concerns? How can they be addressed by the station?

RADIO CLUB PROJECTS, COMMUNITY PROJECTS

Several types of projects are carried out by members of the radio listening clubs. They can be family or individual achievements dealing with hygiene, vegetable gardens, or fruit trees surrounding a house. Other projects are initiated by all the club's members.

The Ingaa radio club, for example, conducted a campaign to combat the lack of soy seeds. Club members decided to plant two gardens with soy seeds belonging to the club. In their activity report they announced:

> The Ingaa radio club is presently reproducing soy seeds, in an effort to share them with other radio clubs and the population during the rainy season. One soy field has already produced a good enough quantity for the next seeding period. Through all of this, we hope to intensify the production and consumption of soy in the Kakwa collective. (Pickery, 1987)

Not all of the radio clubs have been successful — some are intensely active while others seem to be in a continual state of crisis. Among the principal reasons for failure, participants mention; hostility of local authorities; unrealistic projects which are undertaken; corruption by the people in charge of the clubs; lack of follow-through on projects; and jealousy among members. It has also been noted that while the radio clubs help make the relationship between Candip and its listeners more dynamic, their success is restricted by the indirect nature of their access to the station.

MINI-STUDIOS

In 1983, mini-studios were developed in order to enable more direct participation by the population through voice recordings. A mini-studio is, "a radio club which operates well, and, due to its central geographic position in relation to other radio clubs, is given a cassette recorder with which its members record voice pieces to send to Bunia, enriching the participatory quality of the programs." (Pickery, 1987) Each mini-studio serves a number of radio clubs. In an area with a strong oral tradition and a very high rate of illiteracy, mini-studios facilitate the direct expression of the population, enabling people to speak directly and in their own way on the radio. Ideas, emotions, and feelings are better expressed by voice than by a text read from a letter from the listener, which lacks the original rhythm and intonation. By 1991 there were a total of 143 mini-studios in the region, serving some 90% of the radio clubs.

Setting up a mini-studio only takes place when a set of specific conditions are met. A radio club must prove itself over several years through its development work and through regular correspondence with the station. Further, it must establish a resource base and distribute a minimum of twelve cassettes per year. Each mini-studio which Candip equips with a cassette recorder finds itself confronted with several new questions. Who should be recorded? What should be recorded? How should the recordings be done?

The cassettes sent by the mini-studios to Radio Candip include different styles of recordings which are incorporated into a variety of program formats. One method uses a technique known as "see-judge-act" which involves recording discussions about the major problems in the village. A selection of the comments made during the discussion are then sent to Candip, which produces a complete programme on the subject. A second type of programme incorporates the radio clubs responses to questionnaires sent out by Candip. In another technique the station determines 60 programme topics for a series of shows called *Développement et Femme-famille* (Development and Family-woman). The mini-studios are urged to choose one topic which interests them, and to send in their comments and points of view. Finally, there is a type of programme that incorporates important news events from the villages.

In addition to interviews, commentaries and reports, the mini-studio contributions include stories, chants, riddles, skits and similar forms that lend themselves well to the art of radio production.

Each of the station's linguistic groups prepares five thirty minute shows each week and the content of these shows comes, in whole or in part, from the letters sent by the radio clubs and the recordings of the mini-studios. In one recording a traditional doctor tells of his experience with a sick child and discusses how it is necessary to overcome wrong beliefs and customs in order to improve health. In another, a mother explains how she cured her son from *kwashiorkor* using soya. She is able to talk about this over the radio as she would to her friends, using the language and images of her community. Listeners identify more readily with the concrete examples of their peers that with the theories, generalisations and abstractions of "experts." As a result, they are more likely to put the newfound knowledge into practice. Through the microphones of the mini-studios, people are able to express themselves in an authentic manner according to their own traditions, customs and cultures and in their own languages. Through the questions and discussions provoked by this form of communication, people's horizons are broadened. Several years ago, an elderly man voiced the following thoughts:

> We used to think that we lived in an unchangeable situation ... Thanks to the radio, we've found out that there are many things that can change. Who would have thought ten years ago, that an elderly person could learn to read and write? The radio has led us to see and understand what's happening at our neighbours' and elsewhere in our country and the world.
>
> The radio enables us to see beyond our small village. It's as if we were travelling all around to see how people live elsewhere. That's how we learn that many things can and should change here with us and that we can make them change ourselves by relying on our own abilities.
>
> Before, we didn't have the intention of expressing ourselves ... Now, we've learned to speak and to say what we think. The radio has steered us onto this new road by asking that we take part in programmes in our own language. We ourselves ask the questions on the radio.
>
> The radio has opened our eyes, ears, and mouths. (Maréchal, 1982)

* * *

DOCUMENTARY SOURCE MATERIAL

Maréchal, L. (1982) *Candip: rapport des activités en 1981*. Unpublished manuscript.

Pickery, Jan (1987) *Dix ans de Radio-Candip au service des populations rurales — 1977-1987*. Unpublished manuscript.

Pickery, Jan (1988) "Rural Radio in Zaire," *Group Media Journal*, Germany, 1988.

5

How KPFA Found a New Home

Bill Thomas

Located in Berkeley, California, KPFA is the grandparent of community radio in the United States. The station was founded by a group of pacifists just after World War II — they called themselves the Pacifica Foundation. Disgusted by the way radio had been used to stir up the passions of war, they were excited by the idea of using the medium to promote peace and community development. KPFA's beginnings as a commercial station were not very successful. Although pacifism was popular with Americans fed up with war, it was not on the agenda of the government or corporate advertisers. Looking for alternatives, the founders decided to ask listeners to "subscribe" to the station, in the same way they would subscribe to a magazine or newspaper. The plan worked. Today the station gets most of its income from listener donations. Most of these are made during on-air "marathons" when programmers put on their best programming and invite listeners to subscribe and support the station.

As well as being the first community station in the United States, KPFA is also one of the largest. It accepts no advertising, not even limited underwriting, but its listener donations and a few other sources give it an annual budget of over a million dollars a year.

There are a lot of stories to be told about KPFA. The station has had many colourful characters, and produced many extraordinary broadcasts. There have been exciting moments of contact with the community and conflict with authority. The Federal Communications Commission and other government agencies have, at various times, tried to revoke the station's broadcast license. But perhaps a pertinent story to tell, because it reflects present issues in community radio in the United States, is the one about how KPFA got a new home.

Over the years, community radio based on the listener-sponsorship model has become known as raggedy radio-on-a-shoestring, where volunteer programmers work from ramshackle studios with equipment held together by alligator clips and threats from the engineer. Some great programmes have been produced under these circumstances, but the stations have always been financially on the edge. To many, being on the edge has become something of a badge of honour, since it proves that you haven't sold out to the American dream of material success.

A visit to KPFA was enough to convince even the most sceptical that material success was not KPFA's objective. Threadbare carpet, dark creaky hallways, offices filled with beat-up furniture, a newsroom sporting antique tape recorders, and heating, cooling and plumbing systems that barely functioned... This was the "nature" of KPFA, and of all community radio in the USA. At a conference of the National Federation of Community Broadcasters in 1985, for example, participants in one workshop debated whether replacing an old, broken sofa (as one station had recently done) destroyed the appropriate community radio atmosphere.

Given this context, it was a shock for many people when KPFA moved into a new building, designed and built especially for them, with new furniture (much of it custom-built) and new fully equipped studios. Was this still a community radio station? And how could a station that always seemed to be struggling to keep going afford this radio palace?

The story begins with a woman who had been a KPFA listener for many years. Like many other listeners, she regularly made small donations. One day she died. Normally, her death would have been noticed by only a few people at the station. Her monthly programme guide would have been returned by the post office, and after some time, when she failed to make any more donations, her name would have been dropped from the membership list. Many of KPFA's original supporters have been getting old, and it's no surprise that some are dying. However, her story was a little different. In her will she left her home to the station. Most listeners don't do that.

The house, although modest, was valuable because it was in the San Francisco Bay Area, where housing is in high demand. In other times, the money from its sale might have gone into the station's operating budget. But when the bequest was made KPFA was very concerned about finding a new home of its own.

Another longtime supporter of the station had died — KPFA's landlord. For years, he had allowed the station to pay a very low rent. The new owners, however, raised the rate mercilessly. The space had never been ideal for a radio station, but at least until that time it had been a bargain. Moving out started to look attractive, but good space at a low price is hard to come by in Berkeley. So the money from the sale of the deceased supporter's house came to represent a special opportunity — the chance to start a new building fund for KPFA.

A little figuring showed that a new home would be an ambitious project. It would take a couple of million dollars, maybe three, to get a new space for the station. To most KPFA people that seemed completely impossible — especially since the money had to be raised from the same group of people, in addition to ongoing operating costs.

They asked a sympathetic research firm to find out for them if it was feasible to try and raise the additional money. The answer that came back was a surprising "yes." The researchers found that there were a number of people who were prepared to donate to a campaign for a KPFA building, and some were willing to make very big donations. They would have been willing to make such donations before, they said, but no one had asked them. "Thousands of dollars?," asked the researchers. "For KPFA," came the response, "sure."

Patricia Scott, KPFA's manager, was key to moving the whole process forward. One observer of the situation claims that this is in part because she is an African-American:

> A lot of those white progressives at KPFA are stuck in the idea that the station isn't authentic or real unless the chair has broken springs and the tension arm on the tape deck is held up by a rubber band. Pat doesn't see why the community shouldn't have as good a facility as they can get — the multinational corporations shouldn't be the only ones with decent equipment.

Others say it has nothing to do with the fact that she is Black — "she's just a very strong leader who wants to move the station forward."

Strong leader or not, the fundraising campaign was intimidating for her as well. At the opening of the new building, she said "On the morning I had to go for the first time to ask someone for $40,000, I had to practice for hours in front of the mirror. When they said yes, I nearly fell off my chair." By the time the building was opened, they had raised $2,272,015, most of it from individuals. Half a million dollars came from non-profit foundations, and about $95,000 from a government programme.

At the opening of the new building, KPFA staff were proud to show visitors the beautiful tables with inlaid wood, custom-made desks, stained glass lampshades, and wrought-iron work — all created with labour donated by local craftspeople. The opening broadcast featured a special piece called *Homage to Pacifica,* written by major American composer Lou Harrison. A computer system links the whole building, and the architects (KPFA fans, accepting a fee much smaller than their work deserved) designed the inner space to facilitate interaction among workers and to express an openness to visitors. There has been a major improvement in the quality of all the studios and their equipment, which now includes an amazing computerized player piano, a Yamaha "Disk-Klavier."

KPFA is not the first community radio station in the U.S. to raise money to move into better quarters. But because of its high profile, the very large amount of money raised, and the striking contrast between the old and new quarters, the move has sparked debate about the definition of community radio and its position in the community.

Many people, among them listeners, volunteers and paid staff, note that KPFA has not compromised any of its principles. The station still strictly refuses to accept any donations from for-profit corporations, it still stands for free speech and political discussion, programmers still play music ignored by the commercial stations, and KPFA still has the most accessible airwaves in town. The new building shows, they say, that if you stick to your principles and really serve your community, you eventually get rewarded. The way in which people, from well-known progressives to everyday working people, aided the campaign, and donated the labour for the many special touches in the building is evidence of this. They argue that KPFA has proven that it is a community institution that people truly care about, and it is being supported as a community radio station should.

Then there are the dissenters. They wonder if KPFA, which has often claimed to be a voice for the poor and humble, is now alienating itself from them. Will people coming to the station feel like they're entering the headquarters of a big corporation? Will they feel uncomfortable, will they speak differently on the air?

The arguments do go deeper than a concern about the quality of facilities. Part of the reason KPFA's move to a new building is a symbolic event for U.S. community radio is that it comes at a time when there is considerable debate amongst community radio practitioners about the direction of their stations. Discussion has focused on audience research, fundraising techniques, and the important area of programming.

Some people argue that not all community radio's traditional approaches are working very well. They hold that if community radio is to fulfil its mission and have a significant impact in the community, these approaches must change. The airwaves may be accessible to community groups, but the air "sound" is not accessible to listeners. Programmes that have good political or cultural concepts may need to be restructured if they are not reaching people. The common "patchwork quilt" programming schedule, with many specialized programmes each aimed at a different audience, is hard for listeners to follow. Stations need to pay much more attention to the quality of program production, or they will drive the audience away. The programming equivalents of cluttered offices and old sofas don't encourage the community to use the station. The listener may be better served by participating in national programmes with better sound quality, rather than producing everything locally. And finally, stations should take full advantage of the data now available from professional audience survey companies (previously restricted to commercial stations) in order to evaluate how they're doing.

Another side of the debate might be represented by the headline of an article in *Current,* which wonders if community radio is "losing its soul" by "going for the numbers." This approach argues that professional audience surveys have a commercial bias and are therefore inappropriate for community radio. Current programme schedules may seem a jumble, but they represent the diversity and richness of the community. In this view, the new tactics that are being proposed are abandoning community radio ideals for bigger audiences and more income.

Its not hard to see why a beautiful, well-appointed new building would crystallize this debate. But, whatever it represents, the station has taken the plunge — they've built and moved. They're also doing audience research and proceeding with a major revision of their programme schedule. Time will tell how these changes will affect the station and its listeners.

* * *

6

Inventing and Experimenting : Radio Centre-Ville

This text is a collage put together from writings of the following friends of Radio Centre-Ville: Evelyne Foy, Eric L'oiseau, Richard Barette and Louise Boivin.

We would like to take you on a tour through the complicated maze of Radio Centre-Ville, a radio station with a past as rich and eventful as its present. The route will begin with some anecdotes about how it all began, followed by a more theoretical dealing of the principles surrounding the station's participatory structure. Finally, we will end with a look at the role of women in the station.

THE RADIO STATION

Radio Centre-Ville, Montréal is a multilingual community radio station. It has been broadcasting in seven languages for more than 15 years. Seven ethnic groups meet every day to produce a wide variety of radio broadcasts. Organized into teams, they work at creating a collective intercultural community project, reflecting a society which is becoming steadily more mixed. The Greek, Portuguese, Chinese, Haitian, Spanish, English and French-speaking communities are brought together every day. Other cultural communities, such as the South-East Asian, Filipino, African, Irish and Arabic communities, also use the airwaves. Radio Centre-Ville contributes, in its own way, to the coexistence of individuals and different cultures within Québec society. More than three hundred volunteers produce all of the station's programming.

THE CITY

Montréal, with a population of one million inhabitants (three million including the greater Montréal region) is a large cosmopolitan city with inhabitants from almost everywhere in the world. The largest city in Québec and the second largest in Canada, Montréal has been one of the most important cities in north-eastern America since the beginning of European colonization.

Francophones form the majority, with anglophones and other ethnic communities representing respectively 15% of the population, although the latter group is steadily increasing in number. Francophones constitute 80% of the total Québec population of six and a half million. It is important to note, however, that Québec is a tiny island in the anglophone ocean of North America. For this reason it has always had to struggle to protect and promote its distinct language and culture.

WHERE DID RADIO CENTRE-VILLE BEGIN?

A huge movement for social change was built in Québec during the 1960s and 1970s. This movement gave birth to a multitude of organizations, ranging from community-based daycare centres, women's centres, youth centres, citizen's action committees, to several groups fighting for the independence of Québec from Canada. The movement also gave rise to many new communication media: neighbourhood newspapers, alternative press networks on a Québec-wide scale, community television and video production groups. Community radio was part of this new network of popular information. It was in this context that Radio Centre-Ville appeared in 1972, the first station in a movement that was to spread all over Québec.

Daniel Lavoie was one of the francophone pioneers of community radio in Québec.

> There weren't very many of us. The social struggle was very important at that time in Montréal: demands for a better quality of life, urban renewal, battles against the demolition of low cost housing. I was working with people fighting against the construction of a highway which was to link the east and west ends of the city; a huge project which would have brought about the demolition of many neighbourhoods in the city centre. There were also the draft-dodgers, American conscien-

tious objectors against the war in Vietnam, who came seeking refuge in Canada. Kevin Cohalen, one of the founders of Radio Centre-Ville was one of these draft-dodgers; he probably brought the idea of alternative radio from the United States, where that kind of radio had existed since 1946, I believe, in California, and which we were unfamiliar with. Hyman Glustein, the other founder of Radio Centre-Ville, was a student at Sir George Williams, which is now Concordia University.

From the beginning, it was a multi-ethnic radio station. That was one of our principles. We played a lot of jazz too, which was a type of music that everyone could relate to. Our ideology was fairly left-wing, of course. We didn't want to copy the straight radio scene. However, it wasn't community radio in the real sense of the term, meaning a station managed by a board of directors elected by a certain community. It was more an "alternative" or "counter-culture" radio, defending citizens rights. A radio station which wasn't out to make money or do business, but to broadcast popular information, unlike the whole mainstream information machine. Democratic structures weren't a priority, a small group of unelected people could run it and do whatever they felt was best. Later on, this brought about some friendly and less friendly free-for-alls...up to the point of threatening the very survival of the radio station.

At first, we broadcast through the cable network with used equipment; army surplus stuff which couldn't have cost very much, an old console like you see in war movies, turntables and old heavy metal microphones...and it worked! It was a heroic era; we broadcast hours and hours, we were always there, but it was tremendously fun. The majority of our programming was in French — that was a principle, established in proportion with the population.

After a hard battle to get a licence, Radio Centre-Ville came on the FM band February 27, 1975, broadcasting with 7.2 watts of power.

The radio found its niche and grew slowly but surely! But we all know that growing isn't a painless experience, and the first growing pains came in 1977. A group of activists demanded that the radio station become participatory, that it conform to the norms of the CRTC,[1] and that it operate with a board of directors elected by a general assembly. The fact that the people making the demands were supported by "orthodox" Marxist activists did not go over well with the people running the radio station, who feared that it would become a kind of propaganda centre. The radio station, which at the time closed its doors for a two week vacation period every summer, was silent for two months that year in order to solve the problem. Finally, the principle of a general assembly was accepted, especially since it was a legal requirement.

Other crises were to come, as is the case with any popular and democratic organization, but the radio station always managed to pull through. Jean-Louis Legault recalls:

> It's not easy to make an organisation like that work. We didn't have the experience, it was something new and we didn't have any precedents. On the other hand, there are good sides; the pleasure of success, solidarity, etc.... Among my favourite memories, these ones come to mind: the big fifth birthday party on the FM band in November of 1980, where, for three days, a huge multi-ethnic party brought 1200 people together for shows of every kind, film presentations, dances... and the programme that Benoit Fauteux hosted, *Au coeur du samedi soir* (In the heart of Saturday night) broadcast live from different bars, presenting jazz, improvisational theatre and other entertainment.

AN INTERCULTURAL RADIO

Programming at Radio Centre-Ville reflects the cultural mosaic of the city where it has its roots. It is made up of broadcasts produced and hosted by members of the cultural communities using their own languages. They participate in the social life of Québec by communicating their own culture, and at the same time, help their compatriots become more aware of Québec and Canadian current events and culture. Listeners benefit from information in their own languages about the new social environment to which they must adapt, and they conserve their cultural origins.

Communication between newly arrived ethnic groups and long established cultural groups promotes, in many ways, a mutual understanding of habits, moral values, and social or philosophical currents of thought. And it clearly allows a more harmonious coexistence of individuals, despite their differences.

Radio Centre-Ville enjoys a special connection with listeners from very different backgrounds, who are often not very well served by the other media. The station acts as a catalyst between communities and the entire cultural and social fabric, which, in turn, has been enriched by the presence of the communities.

First and foremost a centre for radio broadcasting, Radio Centre-Ville is also a centre for meeting and exchanging ideas and social and cultural experiences. Radio Centre-Ville promotes new cultural currents, such as world-beat music. It welcomes and offers radio production training to anyone who wants to take part and offers a forum to community groups and cultural organizations.

Also contributing to the richness of Radio Centre-Ville are the special events that it broadcasts or that it organizes itself. Because of its contact with the countries of origin of its members, historic events are covered in a special manner on the Radio Centre-Ville airwaves. The station's coverage of events in Haiti is filled with the insight of volunteer journalists from that country. On some occasions, such as elections in Chile or El Salvador, the station might send a correspondent to prepare live reports in both Spanish and French. At other times, we arrange simultaneous broadcasts with sister stations in other countries. Among our solidarity programmes are: specials on the Palestinian question, broadcasts produced weekly behind the walls of a penitentiary with the participation of the prisoners, solidarity programmes with Radio Venceremos and Radio Farabundo Martí in El Salvador, and others for fundraising after natural disasters in Chile and Colombia. All of these examples reflect the human and cultural variety at Radio Centre-Ville.

PARTICIPATORY RADIO

How does participation work at Radio Centre-Ville? Richard Barette, ex-director of francophone programming at the station and a long-time participant gives us his ideas about these questions.[2]

> Inventing and experimenting with new methods of managing activities, different than that of pyramidal organization are, of course, arduous tasks, because they require learning new ways of operating. The best intentions fail most often because of difficulties in putting into practice a genuine and durable collective operation, supported by real participation in decision-making, the sharing of responsibilities and the effective carrying out of projects. Do we want a society that

uses communication techniques to reinforce rigidity and authority, which is the model of the dominant culture or, on the contrary, do we want to see freedom, responsibility and fellowship grow?

Radio Centre-Ville is, by definition, a communication tool at the service of individuals and groups to promote fellowship, quality of life, creativity, local democracy and cultural identity. It is a response to the difficulty of finding identity, communicating, and participating in decision making. It also wishes to respond to the specific needs of its target audience: the working class, newcomers to the country and organizations defending citizens interests. To reach its objectives, Centre-Ville must therefore count on the cooperation of its listeners in order to avoid isolating itself from the real needs of its milieu. To do this, it has developed an operating structure which puts into practice a participatory type of management.

Participation at Radio Centre-Ville has its own particularities due to the nature of the station itself: community-based but also and especially multilingual and multi-ethnic. Accordingly, participation at Radio Centre-Ville depends on membership in one of seven production teams. The participatory system of management is built around these autonomous production teams.

Participating in the management of Radio Centre-Ville means giving up the possibility of staying on the sidelines and comfortably criticizing those who run the station, those who are up front. Participation means expressing personal opinions, complying with group constraints, and supporting decisions.

In many organizations of this kind, one often hears questions such as: Who decides? Who is in control? Who should I support? Who is right? Who will be responsible for failures? A participatory type of management cannot be imposed, without preparation, on people who have not been trained: it requires a certain apprenticeship of all individuals involved.

Good intentions are not enough to ensure that the target population and groups participate in the production of radio broadcasts. These groups must take control of the means of communication by participating in the management and decision making process. In this way, they manage the complete production process of the station.

ORGANIZATION CHART

1) The General Assembly is made up of members of each of the production teams, who are members in good standing of the station.
2) Individual members are those who accept the principles of Radio Centre-Ville and who have participated for a period of three months during the six months preceding the date of the request for membership status. They must belong to one of the seven production teams of Radio Centre-Ville and demonstrate their capacity for teamwork.
3) Organizational members, as well as having the same obligations as individual members, must produce at least 30 minutes of air time per month during the month preceding the request for membership.
4) The Membership Committee, formed of four station members, regularly organizes sessions for inter-team initiation of new volunteers. It grants membership status and may withdraw it on recommendation of the production team.
5) The Board of Directors is made up of 15 members of the station: eight are elected by the general assembly. Each of the seven production teams nominates one candidate for the remaining seven seats. The nominations are ratified by the General Assembly.
6) The Hiring Committee is made up of three representatives of the Board of Directors and makes recommendations to the Board in matters concerning the hiring of paid workers at the station. It is also responsible for all employment relations at Radio Centre-Ville.
7) The Production Teams are the basic units responsible for a certain number of hours of broadcasting per week, as defined by the station. Production Teams are responsible for:
   - job organization
   - broadcast content
   - reception of proposals for programmes within their broadcast time
   - election of their candidate to the Board of Directors
   - advertising sales during their broadcast time
8) The Inter-team Production Committee is made up of a representative named by each production team. Its tasks include:
   - production, promotion and/or broadcast
   - inter-team special interest projects or programmes
   - important projects for one or more production teams, with the approval and collaboration of those in charge of programming and with the promotion of the team or teams

PUTTING THEORY INTO PRACTICE

This theoretical vision of participation inevitably becomes reality through its successes and failures. How can a radio station, which is really seven radio stations with seven production teams, become more accessible? How can genuine communication be established between groups with such different cultures and ways of doing things in a manner that keeps each production team from becoming "ghettoized?" How can the concerns of newcomers be included in the socio-political debates of the *Québécois,* and how can they participate in these debates? How can broadcasts based exclusively in folklore and the nostalgia for countries of origin be avoided? How can the concerns of recently arrived cultural communities be reflected and a real intercultural project developed? How can the interest of youth be raised? How can women be assured a genuine role in these debates?

One project, *Ondes de Femmes* (Women's Waves), has recently gone on the air. It is an attempt to open up the airwaves to women of diverse cultural origin and may provide some answers to the above questions.

ONDES DE FEMMES

Louise Boivin is the former director of Centre-Ville's news room. She is now coordinator of the *Ondes de femmes* project. This is how she described her work:

> The *Ondes de femmes* project was begun because we noticed a low representation of women and groups of women in the production teams at Radio Centre-Ville. Sometimes what appears to be equal representation of women hides the fact that there is a reproduction of traditional roles inside the teams. Women are limited to jobs such as answering the telephone, cleaning up the premises and taking minutes of meetings. Few women are hosts, producers or technicians. Immigrant women are doubly exposed to these difficult conditions.
>
> A radio which wishes to be alternative and community has to prioritize the representation and equal participation of women and their organisations in its programming and its structures. Our declaration of principles clearly affirms that we support collective action to transform society in favour of the marginalized sectors, of which women, unfortunately, all too often form a part.

Women from approximately one hundred women's groups and community and ethnic organizations were invited to participate in the *Ondes de femmes project*. The reaction was so positive that two months later, about fifty women shared in the production of twenty broadcasts in French, Spanish, Creole and Chinese. Intensive training sessions have been organized and a support structure has been set up for the first broadcasts. Links between the women are maintained through monthly meetings, and a weekly information bulletin circulates among them. Participating organizations represent women from all over the world. Many communities which were not already represented at Radio Centre-Ville, or which did not already have women producers, participated in the project. The themes discussed in the programmes are freely chosen by the participants and deal with women's rights generally, as well as with specific problems such as conjugal violence, employment, culture shock and integration.

* * *

The economic crisis, the evolution towards an increasingly intercultural society and the State's disengagement from social programmes means that, more than ever, solidarity is a necessary aspect of our communities. Community radio still has its "raison d'être." As a Radio Centre-Ville document puts it: "We must return to the community, radio has to go to the people. Communities have fewer resources and there is an enormous amount of work to be done. Radio must help them communicate. We have to encourage cultural exchange." Radio Centre-Ville, twenty years strong, still has many challenges to meet.

* * *

NOTES

1. The Canadian Radio-Television and Telecommunications Commission is the federal government body responsible for regulating broadcasting. CRTC regulations require that community radio stations be owned, managed and programmed by members of the community at large.

2. Extracts from a text by Richard Barette in the *Guide de la Radio communautaire au Québec* (Guide to community radio in Québec), Association des radiodiffuseurs communautaires du Québec, ARCQ, 1984.

PART II: CONFLICT

Access to the media by organizations demanding change is most restricted in times of social conflict. Government imposed censorship, threats and assasinations of journalists, and the media's own hostility toward change can all work to exclude certain perspectives from the public forum.

Alternative forms of radio are often able to circumvent this information blockade. This is partially due to radio's ability to reach many people inexpensively, making it an affordable communications tool for social movements. However, a second reason is that the medium offers a degree of flexibility which allows it to cross social, physical and political space with fewer restrictions than other media.

On the social level, radio is accessible by people with varying degrees of education and can be used by literate and illiterate people alike — a characteristic that is as important in inner-city United States as it is in rural Haiti.

On the physical level, radio signals easily cross distances and permit instant communication. This same characteristic also allows radio to cross political boundaries, bypassing government restrictions and regulations.

The following pages recount how radio has been used by five social movements involved in conflicts as varied as an eleven year war for national liberation and the endless struggle against violence against women.

7

The Stubborn Izote[1] Flower

José Ignacio López Vigil

Who hasn't heard of Radio Venceremos, the official voice for the FMLN, the Farabundo Martí National Liberation Front? This guerrilla radio station, whose name means "we will win," stood by the side of the Salvadorean people and broadcast their struggle during eleven interminable years. Quite a record for pirate radio. In such a minuscule country as El Salvador — 21,000 square kilometres — and against an army supplied with the latest in sophisticated weaponry by the United States, the resistance work of Venceremos is a heroic and incredible feat.

In the book The Thousand and One Stories of Radio Venceremos[2], *José Ignacio López Vigil recounts the stories of those involved with Venceremos: how their first broadcasts originated from bomb shelters under the rain of 500 pound bombs, how they recorded reports from the frontlines, the jokes played on gringo radio engineers, the shooting down of the helicopter which carried Monterrosa, the Rambo of the Salvadorean Army, where he carried away like a trophy what appeared to be a Venceremos transmitter but which actually housed eight sticks of dynamite. Dozens of vivid anecdotes recounted by people who produced radio with one hand on the microphone and the other on a gun.*

The following chapter is a selection from the book. It tells the story of Radio Venceremos' role in forcing negotiations, a decisive moment leading to the recent signing of the peace agreements. Based on actual conversations with FMLN guerillas, the text is replete with Salvadorean slang and vulgarities. As the author states, neither the guerrillas nor the soldiers are wont to speak with dictionaries.

This particular chapter proved prophetic. In its concluding paragraph, one of the founders of Venceremos imagines himself able to conduct interviews openly in the working class districts of the capital. Prophetic, because this did indeed happen. On January 16, 1992 following the peace accord signed between the FMLN and the ARENA[3] government, the compañeros *set their transmitter on the roof of the Metropolitan Cathedral of San Salvador. The legendary guerrilla broadcaster*

Santiago[4] transmitted live from the Civic Plaza, with the noisy background of the huge crowd celebrating the victory of the people. The people had fought for peace. And Venceremos had gained legal status after so many years of broadcasting its message of freedom from the mountains of Morazán.

* * *

Manolo[5] gave us the news:

— The FMLN Commanders have decided to launch an offensive, the heaviest in this whole war.
— When?
— Soon.

After almost ten years, there are more than enough reasons to want to put an end to the war. The country is worn out and in ruins. People want peace. We do, too. We don't want to make a profession out of being guerrilla fighters or living in the hills. The world is changing, and that drives you toward solving conflicts through negotiations. But neither Duarte nor, much less, the Army's High Command is going to negotiate anything if we don't put military pressure on them. That's the only thing they understand.

— We're going to take the war to the cities, continued Manolo. We're going to take all the experience we've accumulated over the years, all available arms, all the men, and all our strength. We'll make a big ball out of all that and stick it in San Salvador. They'll have to understand or burst.

That was towards the end of '88, around September. They entrusted us at Venceremos with carrying out a campaign aimed at mentally preparing our soldiers for an offensive without retreat, so we formed a propaganda commission and started to rack our brains for the slogan.

— For social justice and democracy, all unite together to fight the oppressors till the final victory! suggested someone, whose name I won't mention.

— That's too long, man. Before you finish pronouncing it, the bombs'll be dropping into your mouth.
— Crush criminal fascism! said somebody else, whose identity I won't reveal either.
— Too heavy.
— Build peace!
— Too cold. Look at the way the Nicaraguans do it: "Everybody all out!" Why can't we invent something that has a little bit of Salvadorean flavour to it?
— Salvadorean? said Santiago. Listen to this: With the finger of unity up the enemy's ass! You can't get much more Salvadorean than that.

We all laughed at the sick joke, but we couldn't get the slogan out. Finally, Maravilla came up with something:

— What does an officer say when he gives the order to storm?
— Stick it to'em!
— Well, that's the best slogan: "Stick it to'em!"
— Doesn't it sound too militaristic?
— Not that much. It's also erotic. When you're dancing, don't you stick it to the girl?
— Stick it to'em and what else?
— Stick it to'em, period. This is all coming to a head, isn't it? So we want to put a final end to this whole thing.

Of love and war, that's what stuck: "Stick it to'em, period!" With that, the feverish preparations began: training for urban commandos, the formation of insurrectional detachments, and concentrated operations on the war fronts. At the radio we were stirring up the fire.

— When? we wanted to find out.
— Soon.

The supplies, the organization, and the entire plan for the offensive were ready. But the right time had to be found, politically speaking. It was going to be a big whack, and the population had to feel that the FMLN had exhausted all chances of doing things with the government by peaceful means.

The elections were drawing near. The gesture was as unexpected as it was audacious: the FMLN's General Commanders made known that they were willing to participate in the elections, provided that they be fair, subject to international supervision, and postponed until October in order to give the FMLN time to carry out a campaign in the same conditions as the other political parties.

The proposal was so logical that even the Gringos accepted it. However, ARENA rejected it outright. After hesitating at first, Duarte[6] went along with ARENA, invoking "constitutional order." As a result of that attitude, a long history of electoral shams, and the promise of another to come, we called on the population to abstain from going to the polls.

The abstentions won those March 19 elections with a total of 62%. But since paper-ballot democracy doesn't take the people's rejection into account, the presidency went to the ARENA candidate, Alfredo Cristiani, who had received slightly over half the votes cast. In other words, Cristiani began to govern with the representation of 17% of voting-aged Salvadoreans.

— What's the story with the offensive? asked our combatants, who'd been left hanging.
— So when?

At Radio Venceremos we were continuing to heat up the atmosphere, but we were getting impatient. The Commanders presented another initiative for a peaceful settlement.

Doesn't Cristiani say that his government is democratic? Then let's sit down and have talks. And they did sit down in Mexico at a high-level meeting, with Shafick Handal and Joaquín Villalobos, from our side. Unfortunately, ARENA sent a second-rate commission with no power to make decisions.

The only thing that resulted from that meeting in September was the decision to hold another one in October, this time in San José, Costa Rica. There it went even worse. Military officers were spying from the second floor of the place where the talks took place so that the government commission wouldn't say or sign anything without first consulting with them.

A few days later, a bomb exploded at the FENASTRAS[7] building, killing Febe Elizabeth, the leader of UNTS[8], and ten other union leaders. There were more and more places being searched and people put in jail, and paramilitary repression against the popular movement increased. It was obvious that Cristiani didn't even have the slightest will to negotiate.

— Get it all ready for November 11, they told us. Now those bastards are going to find out what the FMLN's made out of!

The offensive was to be launched against the country's five major cities: San Salvador, Santa Ana, San Miguel, Zacatecoluca, and Usulután. In addition to these strategical priorities, there would be a whole bunch of smaller military efforts.

Venceremos was going to stay up there in Morazán, broadcasting from an underground station. Only a small group of us would remain, practically without any security, because the war was going to be carried on down in the south and nobody was going to bother with us. Not even the buzzards would be flying overhead.

November 11 arrived. We checked the connections and went over the whole transmitting and audio system for the umpteenth time to make sure that absolutely nothing would go wrong. The sun went down. We were underground, sitting behind the microphones, surrounded by little light bulbs, and with all the military radios turned on. Just a few minutes before eight, Atilio[9] called us:

— We're on the bucking bronco, he told us. There's no turning back now.
— Any orders? we asked him.
— If you know how to pray, do it.

You wouldn't believe it without having seen it. On Saturday, November 11, in the district of Colonia Zacamil, there was a wedding in which the bride, dressed in white, the groom, in coat and tie, the best man and bridesmaid, guests, musicians, and drunks were all urban commandos. The guns were wrapped up in gift boxes. It was all a trick to bring people together, distribute arms, and take over a sector of the city.

In Mejicanos there was a soccer game where the 11 players on each team, the referees, onlookers, women selling crushed ice, and the bus they came and left on were all part of a disguised movement of troops designed to take over that sector.

At a house in Colonia Metrópoli, the couples started to arrive at five in the afternoon. They were young men and women who'd shown up holding each other's arms, laughing, and making way for the cars that were leaving and returning full of guns. Those weapons still hadn't been oiled because they'd just come out of the caches where they'd been kept for months.

In that house 46 young people came together from different neighbourhoods. They were university students, union members, and all sorts of individuals. Three of them had combat experience. The rest had never touched a pistol in their lives. They'd been preparing with courses, radio programmes, and pamphlets, but they'd never had a shoot-out with anybody. At six in the afternoon, those in charge began to hand them their hardware and give them basic instructions about its use.

A National Police vehicle pulled up and parked across the street from the house. The cops got out and began to patrol the street.

— The police! warned one of the young men. Either somebody squealed to them, or we've got the worst fucking luck we could.

Comandante Choco, who was responsible for that group, didn't stop smiling when the police knocked at the door.

— Good evening, said the policeman.
— Good evening, Choco answered.
— Look, friend, could you give us a little water?
— Of course, just a second.

Inside, in the next room, 46 urban commandos were oiling a pile of guns. Had a neighbour noticed something? Was there an informer? But the police drank their water and took off without so much as sticking their heads inside the door. Maybe they suspected something and didn't want to get themselves into a fight when it was almost time to change shifts and they were about to go home.

At eight in the evening, Choco brought all the new combatants together:

— The time has come, guys. Everybody into the street!

The door opened, and the whole flock of guerrillas rushed out, each with a brand-new gun, to take over the sector. This would be their first encounter with the cops, whose truck was still parked only a few blocks away.

And with that, all hell broke loose. This was the biggest bang in ten years of war. Thousands of men and women poured out into the streets of San Salvador. They opened fire in the northern neighbourhoods, dug trenches, put up barricades, and completely disconcerted the Army, which had smelled something coming and prepared a large operation in Guazapa to keep our troops from entering the city.

But we were already inside! The FMLN was fighting in Colonia Zacamil, Mejicanos, Ciudad Delgado, Cuscatancingo, Soyapango, and Ayutuxtepeque. The guerrillas were attacking the capital of the country!

In San Salvador, the offensive began with a simultaneous attack on 50 enemy positions, including the Army's General Headquarters and Cristiani's own residence. However, at Venceremos we were playing dumb. We said that we'd received news of "some attacks" here and there. We didn't want to kick up a storm or use the word "offensive" until we saw how the wheel was turning. That way, if something went wrong and they drove us out of San Salvador that same night, we could just not make much of a fuss about what was happening.

But other stations didn't swallow it. At 8:15, Radio KL set off its alarm:

> *Extra, extra! Heavy fighting is taking place in the northern area of the capital. Practically all the working-class neighbourhoods have become the theatre of one of the FMLN's most violent onslaughts.... We have also received information from Zacatecoluca, where the guerrillas have attacked....*

The Armed Forces High Command didn't believe that mere skirmishes were taking place, either. Exactly two hours after the attacks began, Ponce[10] publicly decreed a state of siege and established a national radio and television emergency network.

On Sunday, the 12th, at 6 a.m., we went on the air like the evening before, without making much noise. A short while later, Atilio gave us the green light:

— The rice is cooked, he said. Start using the word "offensive."

Now everyone was referring to the big FMLN offensive. The guerrillas had always attacked at night and withdrawn before daybreak, but now the sun was high in the sky and our people were still going at it in the streets of San Salvador, Zacatecoluca, Usulután, downtown San Miguel....

The urban commandos who'd opened fire from within had now been joined by the FMLN's real military force, the peasant columns that had taken advantage of the Army's disorder and entered the cities. There was fighting going on in every department of the country. That's when Venceremos let loose.

We'd set up three stalls with radio equipment to receive immediate military information from all our command posts. Facundo, Carmelo, and Dimas were informing. From every corner of the country, dozens of radio operators were sending us war reports with their 40-meter orange units, the famous *Spilsburys.*

Their signals were transmitted to any one of our three reception stalls, which were far away from each other to avoid interference. There was a radio operator in each stall, and, next to her, a messenger, a boy with wings on his feet.

The radio operator had pieces of paper already cut and ready, with their sheets of carbon paper. Every piece of news was written in three copies. As the information came in, she'd write it down as fast as she could, keeping one copy for herself and giving the other two to the runner.

Then the kid would take off like a bullet for the underground studio. At the entrance, before jumping into the hole, he'd give a copy to the girl who was sitting at the entrance and classifying the reports into fourteen folders, one for each of El Salvador's departments. All out of breath, the boy would reach the end of the shelter, where we were broadcasting. There Santiago grabbed the piece of paper and immediately turned on the microphone:

> *Just minutes ago, at 10:35 a.m., our forces destroyed an armoured tank on the corner of...*

We had a fourth stall, the special one, for communication with other countries. Don't ask me how or where because I can't tell you. Let's just say that it's where the military thugs would never imagine. We'd set up

Maravilla in an office with telephones, computers, and all that modern shit. Just as day was breaking, Maravilla would call us on a direct channel:

> — This is Mouse calling. Look, I've got a *New York Times* editorial that's just come by fax. Here it goes; I'll translate it for you.

Incredible! At six in the morning, a contact would buy the paper in New York. At 6:05, he was faxing it to Maravilla's office. At 6:10, Maravilla was translating it to us on a secret band, and, less than a quarter of an hour later, we were discussing it on Venceremos.

Down in our pit in Morazán, we were receiving opinions from the US press sooner than a Gringo sitting in his office in Manhattan! We also received news from the Spanish and German press. We were monitoring all the important TV news programmes in the world via satellite. Since we expected the government to decree a state of emergency and a put a gag on information, Maravilla spent his time watching foreign TV with his dish antenna. Later, he'd lend us his eyes.

> *Marvin, I'm watching the troops from the Atlcatl Battalion all crowded together around the Army's General Headquarters building. They're wearing camouflage uniforms, and their faces are painted. You can tell they're very nervous, and they don't know where to point their guns....*

Maravilla would narrate in minute detail everything he was picking up over NBC or CBS, and we'd report it as if we were right in San Salvador. That's how that fantastic link worked.

On Monday we started to broadcast straight from six in the morning until eleven at night. There were only four of us announcers, and the broadcasts were exhausting marathons. We did shifts of six and eight hours, which left Santiago voiceless and loosened Leti's tongue. They ruined my nerves and finished training Herbert, the Venceremos rookie who still didn't have too much improvising ability.

Everything had to be improvised. There was no time to scratch your head. The news showed up, and you had to make your commentary right on the spot. Santiago and I would be talking and forgetting about the mike, as if we had our audience in front of us.

At other times, we'd challenge members of the high society, summoning them by name to abandon their mansions. One afternoon, Santiago started to pick on William Walker, the *gringo* ambassador in El Salvador and namesake of the other swine from the last century:[11]

> *Aren't you ashamed, Mr. Walker?....In what school did you learn your diplomacy?*

He raked him over so hard, and the Ambassador was so upset, that the US State Department sent a message to the FMLN through our Political-Diplomatic Commission:

— Let's make a deal. Stop insulting our personnel, and we'll take the "terrorist" label off you.

Alright. The next day we held Santiago back, and they removed that little nickname. Venceremos had them concerned because, at that time, even the deaf were listening to it.

We'd never had so many listeners in all our ten years. People have told me that you could go to Metrocentro[12] and hear Venceremos at full blast in the stores. We were monitored without interruption by the middle class, the press, the enemy, the *gringos*, and even Cadena Cuscatlán, which all the stations in the country had to stay hooked up with. You'd hear Santiago informing that we'd just taken such and such a place, and, a couple of minutes later, the Cuscatlán commentator would furiously deny it.

We tried out new formats, which increased our number of listeners: news bulletins every hour, sketches, comic dialogues, and jingles based on well-known music, like this little rumba by María Cristina:

> *Freddy Cristiani can't govern*
> *Because I cut off,*
> *I cut off all his lights.*
> *Everybody join in with*
> *Sabotage and we'll win fast.*
> *Stick it to'em, period!*

I'm not going to tell you what people said, but rather what they did. On the night of the 11th, when the guerrillas arrived, people went out to support them, but still with a bit of fear. The next day there were more of them. By the fourth day, everybody was busy making food for them and giving them clothes. One young guerrilla said to a lady:

— Ma'am, would you happen to have an old pair of pants that you could lend me, something that your husband doesn't wear anymore? I'd just need'em until my uniform dries. I've been sleeping here in the trench with wet clothes for two nights now.

Just with that, the news travelled all around my community and the neighbouring ones, and a commission was formed in each district to provide clothing. People would show up with tons of clothes and say:

— For the guerrillas!

Even the poorest of people came out with their little dress, skirt, panties, underpants, socks, and all sorts of stuff for the guerrillas. And all that guy had needed was one pair of dry pants! But the neighbours got together and built up a mountain of clothes.

People were happy. We'd been told that those who were fighting were foreigners: Nicaraguans, Cubans, Vietnamese, and from I don't know where else. So we were watching out for the way they looked, right? And when people saw them come marching in, they'd say: hey, so and so. They were old friends or family whom they hadn't seen for years. And they gave each other big hugs.

— Nephew, where did you come from?
— Brother-in-law, we thought you were dead!

So it turned out that the so-called foreigners were from our neighbourhoods. Only the doctor, a big white fellow, had the look of a foreigner to us. The rest of them were all perfect Indians, just like us. You know what I mean?

Something special happened with that guerrilla doctor. Since nobody in our neighbourhoods has money to pay for health care, people started to hang around when they found out that a doctor and a nurse were there.

— What's wrong with the little girl, ma'am?

— She's got a bit of a fever, Doctor. You know, she didn't even sleep a wink last night.
— Come on over here.

They took her into the little shelter they'd set up. It was a kind of field hospital. By the time she came out, another little girl was waiting. And the guerrilla doctor began to treat all the sick people in the area. There were people with diarrhea, bad nerves, epileptic fits, people with so many ailments that the poor doctor couldn't even take care of his wounded companions anymore because he was too busy seeing the people from the neighbourhood. People were grateful, and they started to take him coffee or tortillas or shoes. Since nobody had any money, they gave the doctor whatever they had.

— No, ma'am. Keep the food for your son. If not, you'll have to bring him back soon to see me again. What he's sick from is hunger.

People started to feel at ease with the guerrillas.

— You can talk with these soldiers, they said. We can have a smoke together. We can take them into our houses to eat. They're not like those other soldiers that make you feel shaky just by looking at you cause you never know how they're gonna fuck you over.

That's the way my neighbours talked. In my neighbourhood we were happy just going to buy things for them at the stores and supermarkets. We'd give them sugar cane and other things so that they could hold out.

More than anything else we hoped that they'd never leave us. As things turned out, it was the other way around. We're the ones who had to run off. When people heard about what the Air Force was doing in Soyapango and Zacamil, about the bombings in areas where there were homes, well then they left in a hurry with whatever they could. People were crying as they left with their little bags, and, when they turned around to see the guerrillas, who'd stayed behind, they said:

— Those poor kids! May God forgive me, but I have to leave.

The planes were already coming in our direction.

On Wednesday, November 15, we were within a hair's breadth of collapsing the Army and winning the war. The working-class neighbourhoods had turned into FMLN strongholds. Each building was a fort. The Army entered with armoured cars and its troops behind them, trying to recover terrain and deplete our supplies, but it succeeded in neither. Instead, as time went by, there were so many neighbours joining us, and the setback to the Army was so accelerated, that on Wednesday evening, fearing a general insurrection, the High Command held an emergency meeting at its General Headquarters.

Many things have been found out about that sinister meeting in which the 30 highest-level Army officers took part. This is where they decided to step up the intensity of the war, no matter what the political cost of the ensuing genocide.

— It's them or us, asserted one of the colonels.

That's where they decided to use the Air Force against the civilian population. Helicopters would use machine-gun fire against the working-class neighbourhoods.

They also decided on a night of long knives: that very night and into the early morning they would murder those they considered to be the brains behind the subversion. At the head of the list were the Jesuit priests from the Central American University (UCA).[13]

It's said that, when the meeting was over, the military officers held each other's hands and prayed together for the success of their crimes. In the macabre circle were a few pairs of *gringo* hands, those belonging to CIA advisors.

I was still half asleep on Thursday, the 16th, when I managed to grasp the crackling news.

— They killed Ellacuría,[14] confirmed Ana Lidia.
— That can't be, I said.

Santiago was stretching and getting ready to start broadcasting. A terrible look came over his face when he found out.

— It's true. They also murdered Segundo Montes and Martín Baró and...

Santiago turned on the mike and began to speak. Since the times of the first offensive back in January of '81, I'd never seen him so indignant or so sad.

> *Here in Morazán, in order to make soup for the guerrillas, the girls who work in the kitchens go out to look for izotes. They cut off their hearts and put them into the pot. But everytime it's cut, the izote shows its incredible instinct for survival. It reproduces immediately. If you go back a month later, you'll see the izote sprouting up again. Even if the machete cuts it off at the roots, the izote always comes back. It always insists stubbornly on blossoming again, on continuing with life.*
>
> *It occurs to us that Ignacio Ellacuría is like those izotes. Martín Baró, Segundo Montes, Amando, Juan Ramón, and Joaquín López are all like the izote flower, stubborn to die and stubborn in their efforts to continue growing.*
>
> *Why do we say this? Because Cristiani didn't think about the fact that all of them were teachers who multiplied their knowledge with the thousands and thousands of young people who studied with them. They multiplied those moral values of Christianity that are so compatible with revolutionary principles. The moral values that these priests communicated are now thousands of seeds. They weren't the brains of subversion. They were part of our national conscience, of the critical and scientific conscience that searched for the roots of the conflict and researched our history, attempting to find the way to peace and national reconciliation.*
>
> *We know that our people will take up this izote flower, which is El Salvador's national symbol. We know the Salvadorean people will raise it in their fists as a symbol of the stubborn will for peace that flowed in the veins of the murdered Jesuit priests. And we know that the day of that victory, which is coming rapidly closer, people will pour into the city squares from all four corners of this nation.*
>
> *These people will raise the izote flower of Ignacio Ellacuría and of the 70,000 Salvadoreans who have died. People will flow into the country's squares with an uproar, like a river during the rainy season, to pay tribute to these brothers of ours who died for the sake of peace, to these brothers who were born in Spain but were more*

> *Salvadorean than their assassins, a pack of criminals with denationalized minds.*
>
> *On the day of that victory, the mothers of the fallen, their brothers and sisters and children will all be there. This struggle has 70,000 martyrs. The barbarianism has affected millions of Salvadoreans: those of us who have lost a brother or a sister or a friend or Ignacio Ellacuría, those of us who have lost Monseñor Romero. On behalf of them, onward towards peace!*
>
> — Santiago, November 19, 1989, On the day of the Jesuits' burial.

They bombed the cities. In San Miguel, the Third Brigade's 105-millimetre cannon barrels were pointed towards the areas where neighbours had taken part in the insurrection. Colonel Vargas gave the order to open fire. The little wooden houses blew into pieces as they were hit by the Army's blindly launched shells. Afterwards, you saw dead children, corpses, and pieces of people trapped in the rubble. Then the helicopters completed the massacre.

They bombed the civilian population indiscriminately. They so thoroughly destroyed San Salvador's working-class districts that we were forced to change our positions. We carried out a manoeuvre during the night and moved into Colonia Escalón.[15]

— Let's see if they bomb these nice little rich people! said Chico[16] as he was setting up his command post in one of the largest mansions that belong to the oligarchy.

The upper-class woman almost fainted when she saw that 30 guerrillas had invaded her house.

— What do you want? What are you looking for here?
— Take it easy, ma'am, said Chico, trying to calm her down. You just carry on your life as usual.
— And what are you going to do?
— For right now, we're gonna eat. We're hungry.
— Here there's no...
— Sure there is. We're not stealing anything here because you've got more than enough food.

— Alright, acquiesced Fufú, as she was going to call the servants.
— No, Chico replied, stopping her. You're the one who's going to cook.
— Me?
— Yes, you.
— How could you?
— This way, even though it's just for a few minutes, you'll get to experience what women go through every day in the kitchen. What do you want, guys?
— Fried eggs!
— Beans!
— Serve them, Chico told her. That's a simple-enough menu, isn't it?

You should've seen the old lady grabbing pots and burning her hands with the grease. But yes she did cook. A woman from the oligarchy served lunch to our guerrilla fighters.

The capture of the Sheraton was directed from that mansion. We attacked the huge hotel because it was the highest point in the neighbourhood, but we didn't know who was inside: none other than Organization of American States (OAS) Secretary General, Joao Baena Soares, who'd travelled to El Salvador in order to find out about the war and ended up experiencing it.

The Sheraton turned into something like the plot of a comic film. On the top floor you had a dozen *gringo* Green Berets barricaded behind mattresses and scared shitless, once they'd found out that guerrillas had slipped into the hotel. On the first floor, Army soldiers were even keeping an eye on the sewer manholes so that the guerrillas couldn't escape from the building. We were there in the middle, competing with a few soldiers to see who could protect Baena Soares the best.

Following several hours of great tension, negotiations got under way. Bishop Rosa Chávez came, in order to ensure the agreements. The OAS Secretary General left the hotel without so much as a scratch. Then our guys and the Army soldiers left.

The last ones to withdraw from the hotel were the fainthearted *gringos*. They went secretly out the back door, covering their faces and carrying little white flags, just in case. They looked horrified by the whole thing, which could only have taken place in the kind of violent country that their Pentagon sponsors.

Back in Morazán, we were able to broadcast everything as if it were live: both the commotion at the Sheraton and the taking of Escalón and the other rich neighbourhoods, which the Army of the rich naturally decided not to bomb. Maravilla used his eyes, and we provided the voices.

We also transmitted news immediately via our network of military-radio operators in other cities where the fighting was just as fierce as in the capital. We hooked up with our fellow station, Farabundo Martí, to inform the world, both near and far, about the most impressive military effort ever carried out by a Latin American guerrilla movement.

After 14 days of offensive, we began to withdraw from San Salvador and the other cities. The ruthlessness of the Air Force had much to do with this decision. If we'd had missiles, it would've been a different story, you know. But we didn't at that time.

We had to explain the order to withdraw to our companions in arms because they wanted to stay there in their positions. However, it wasn't of much use to hold onto trenches in bombed-out neighbourhoods that the civilians had evacuated. And, anyway, we'd won the main battle: strategically speaking, we'd turned around an apparently stalemated war.

See you in San Salvador!

No one would've bet a dime on us before the offensive. The huge battles that we'd waged in the countryside weren't being seen in the city. When we stopped transportation or blew up high-tension pylons, we were affecting the entire population, but sabotage is something very different from flying bullets.

People hadn't really felt the war in San Salvador. So, out of sight, out of mind and lots of propaganda in your head. Drop by drop, news item by news item, throughout their mass media, they told about what hadn't happened and omitted what had. They portrayed the FMLN as a weakened force, and they ended up believing their own lies: "They're barely a handful of guerrillas living along the Honduran border. They're deserting; they don't have any weapons; they've got nobody behind them...."

That's why we weren't making any progress in the negotiations. Nobody wants to negotiate with the dying. If the guerrillas are dying out, let's put them off until they fade away all by themselves.

What went on in the Mexico and San José talks? Just a lot of blab. Cristiani sent his commissions only to stall for time and improve his government's international image. The talks also helped the US Congress to justify further military aid, which would contribute, finally, or so they thought, to liquidating the remaining pockets of guerrilla fighters. So the *gringos* also thought that they were giving us the full count of ten.

The November offensive changed all that. Who would have thought that we were capable of laying siege to the capital for almost a month? When had an oligarch from Colonia Escalón ever imagined that he'd be seeing military clashes on his own block?

Now they've smelled powder and heard explosions. Not even their grandmothers still believe the tale that we're just a thimbleful of guerrillas brooding in the hills. We took the war into the cities and right into the very heart of the nation's existence.

We did lose 401 lives. One by one, we read every name over Venceremos, starting with Commander Dimas Rodríguez. The great majority of our casualties were men and women who had just joined our ranks and hadn't had much combat experience.

On one hand, the FMLN's military structure remained intact. On the other hand, the Army suffered its worst defeat in all the years of the war. According to confirmed data, the Army lost nearly 3,000 men. Another 3,000 soldiers and recruits deserted during the offensive. In January, with rumours circulating about a second offensive, 1,300 more soldiers ran away from the barracks.

We strengthened ourselves. We now have more urban commandos than ever before, more unit leaders, hundreds of young people who withdrew with us, and thousands of neighbours there in their little houses and apartment blocks, already trained and waiting for the next call.

The political victory was even more important than the military success. The offensive forced the ruling fascist Army to remove its mask. In its desperation, the Army had no qualms about assassinating the Jesuits and bombing civilians, right in front of international journalists and UN and OAS representatives.

Above all, the offensive forced the negotiations. That's what was intended: to wipe the smirk off Cristiani's face and, mainly, to sit the US representatives down for talks. They're the decisive counterparts in all this affair. They're the owners of the circus. Now even Thurman[17] has stated that the Salvadorean Army "cannot defeat the FMLN." At least they understood that much.

In San José, when we raised the question of purging the Armed Forces, Larios[18] termed that condition as absurd and ridiculous. Now it's the main item on the agenda. When we brought up the agrarian reform and reforms in the judicial system, they simply paid no attention to us. Now it's Cristiani himself who's talking about negotiations. Fine. It was via military action that we dispensed with a military solution to the war. That was the greatest benefit of the offensive.

Sometimes, as if they were insane, the power elite lose their sense of reality and go back into an imaginary world. They're encouraged by the invasion of Panama and the Sandinista electoral defeat in Nicaragua. They pluck up their courage with the fall of Eastern Europe, and they get all excited about these things. They're confusing apples and oranges, and they're dreaming about a rapid and repressive solution in El Salvador.

Well, a mule only understands the language of a stick, so, if November's offensive wasn't enough, we'll prepare three more for them. Unfortunately, we have to maintain the threat of a new offensive in order to ensure the negotiations.

Venceremos is included in the negotiating agenda. So they want us to go back to civilian life? We'll do it, but with our entire communication apparatus; that's to say, with the means to take part in public debate.

They want us to register for truly free elections, with full guarantees? Then, one of the things that we should guarantee is the freedom to communicate our thinking. In other words, a station hidden in the hills doesn't fit our needs well enough anymore. Venceremos has already done its time as a guerrilla station. Because of the country's current political situation, the developments of the war, and the new state of affairs in the rest of the world, we need Venceremos to come legally out in the open.

We have to rid the radio of its buzzing by obtaining a broadcasting license and we have to stop using barbed wire antennas. We have a right to debate our viewpoints in public and to use the media for that purpose on an equal footing with the country's other political forces.

The time has come for the FMLN and its radio station to enter into public and legal existence and to vie for power on those terms. That's what we're proposing: Radio Venceremos in San Salvador, with its doors open to the public. Are these mad ravings, or natural demands in a country where people in arms have won the right to democratize?

What are we going to do in San Salvador? The idea isn't to transplant our guerrilla programming to the capital. In order to respond to the new challenge, we have to make a tremendous change in our style and the way that we communicate.

* * *

We can't frankly say that we've attracted the greatest number of listeners in these last few years. Why not? The problem isn't how correct you are in what you're saying, but whether or not you can be heard. Technically speaking, we've had weak reception and strong interference. It's true that our programming hasn't been the best, either.

But it's also true that the message from Venceremos goes beyond the simple contents of what's being said. It's the fact that it exists, that it's there. If it's there, it's because they're strong, because they hold terrain, because they've got people's support.

When the first big operation was launched against Morazán, the objective was to resist, to show that there was territory being defended by the FMLN and that those zones were under our control. The radio's first political message consisted of letting our friends and the enemy know that we were there, just shouting or saying any damned thing, but there we were. And we spent those days broadcasting under mortar fire.

On countless occasions we've continued broadcasting underground, under the rain, with the soldiers nearby, with helicopters overhead, and with the greatest determination to go on the air ever displayed by a radio station anywhere in the world. Can you imagine what it means to keep a station like this one going for ten years in a tiny little country like ours with a full-scale war?

With your fingers you can count the times we've missed going on the air, and some of those times it was our own decision not to have a programme. When the station went dead in '84, it was in order to kill Domingo Monterrosa, and we had to send notice to all the guerrilla fronts so that they wouldn't be demoralized by our silence.

Now we're in a new stage. The present challenge is much more than just resisting: it's to compete. What's your message? What are you going to say? How can you reach everyone: guerrillas and non-guerrillas, peasants and city dwellers, our militants and those who aren't convinced? Especially those who aren't convinced.

So it's time to change, to make changes in everything: from increasing our broadcasting power and improving our signal to opening up our minds. What's done is done. Was it the best that could have been done or wasn't it? It was at a different point in the war. I guess Madonna wouldn't have been of much use to us when we were moving to take over Cacahuatique. But now the winds have changed.

Where should we start? It's fine to play rock and popular music, but we need to do more than that. If we want to compete in the city, we have to deal with city themes and talk about the things the people are talking about. The war was making us one dimensional. We've put blinders on ourselves, and we only talk about the political and economic aspects of things and about the macroproblems affecting workers.

But that same worker who's listening to us has a family, likes soccer, and goes drinking with his buddy. More than the union, he's concerned about the bastard who's prowling around his wife when he goes off to his meetings.

We have to talk about all those things, about people's everyday life. And it's starting there, with the price of milk, or with the Firpo team beating Alianza, that we have to put together our programming so that it's closer to and more captivating for the San Salvador listeners. For example, you've got the case of La Tencha, who reflects the way we speak and the sexual humour that we Salvadoreans so enjoy. Atilio came a few days ago, and he asked me:

— What's up? How are the *Renatos*[19] doing?
— Damned good. La Tencha's programme has made a big hit.
— How's the reception in the city?
— It's getting there. It reaches the fronts, too.
— Give them all the support you can. Do you know what I mean? In addition to the programme, there's the question of unity with them.

Look at the way life changes! Roque Dalton would be pleased to hear that the guys from the *Resistencia Nacional* are making one of the most popular programmes on Venceremos. I was thinking of that when I sat down to have a talk with Fermán Cienfuegos.[20]

— Congratulations for La Tencha, I said to him.
— Really?
— Really.

— I told them not to politicize the programme too much, that it was better to do it more along the lines of daily life. With short steps you get where you're going faster, don't you think?

Another principle is the conviction that the truth cannot be imposed, even if it is true. We should avoid all forms of indoctrination that reduce truth to nothing more than slogans or that hide or manipulate information. At times, in order to do things the easy way, to save time, or out of impatience, we have taken the misleading shortcut of indoctrination.

But the road to a truth that is shared, shown, and discovered through participation is always more revolutionary. It is a long and difficult road, but it is the road. Whoever imposes and indoctrinates does not triumph. Triumph only comes when someone is convinced.

— Fermán Cienfuegos, *Propaganda, Democracy, and Revolution,* July 1989.

Who will be able to speak on Venceremos? Anyone, except for the dead. If we're going to have a pluralistic model, then we should accept that same pluralism in the communication of ideas. We want the culture of debate to prevail over the stupidity of censorship in our country. We want to bring democracy to the microphones.

Let Venceremos in San Salvador be the best and broadest forum for all social sectors and all political positions: right, left, and centre. Listen and draw your own conclusions. If the others argue better than we do, they'll force us to deepen our analyses and formulate the FMLN's project better and more creatively.

This political and ideological pluralism does not respond to fashion or, much less, to outside pressure. Neither did the enemy force us to allow for it nor did our friends from fellow countries lay down conditions so that we would accept it.

It's because we believe in it. We believe because we've opened our eyes and seen what this whole process in El Salvador has been. Those who've made this revolution are Christians and Marxists, Social Democrats and Christian Democrats. All of them have been making sacrifices, sticking their necks out, and firing bullets. They've all been part of the vanguard, not just the guerrillas.

In a revolutionary model, freedom of expression is obviously needed in order to maintain an internal social balance. The present context demands a political defense that can debate and educate the masses, that can teach them to reflect and defend their long-term project. This cannot be done without opposition or without learning about the adversary's plans.

This debate forces us to elaborate on and deepen the analysis of our revolutionary position if we are to save it from ideological dogmatism and paralysis. It is fundamental to provide for a professional, critical, and independent brand of journalism and to put an end to the oligarchy's exclusive ownership of mass media, but without violating freedom of expression.

— Joaquín Villalobos, *Perspectives for Victory and the Revolutionary Project,* March 1989.

* * *

Venceremos originated in the context of the war. It has accompanied this exaggeratedly heroic struggle right from the first day and throughout its ten years. Our pieces of equipment have been used to inform, debate, provide political direction, and even as strategical weapons with eight sticks of dynamite inside them. Now these same pieces of equipment have become bargaining chips at the negotiating table.

By the time this book comes out, we'll probably be set up in San Salvador. Inevitably, such a democratic opening has to occur. We had to win a right to legality by acting outside the law. Just like the Salvadorean people themselves, our station had no other place but the mountains where it could exercise its rights and make its voice heard.

I can already see myself doing interviews in Colonia Zacamil, taping short soap operas in the markets, and offering time over these still-secret mikes to the poor people in the working-class districts. People who before had only Monseñor Romero's voice to speak for them will soon be able to speak for themselves. Let's listen to those who've spent years and centuries waiting in the line of history to speak their mind.

* * *

NOTES

1. The izote is El Salvador's national flower. It is edible and used in many traditional dishes.
2. UCA Editores, San Salvador 1991.
3. ARENA: Alianza Republicana Nacionalista, the right-wing that is currently in power in El Salvador.
4. Santiago: First host and founder of Radio Venceremos.
5. Manolo: Captain Ramón Emilio Mena Sandoval, joined the guerrillas following the take over of the Santa Ana barracks during the first major guerrilla offensive on January 10, 1981.
6. José Napoleón Duarte, Christian-Democrat, a former President of El Salvador.
7. FENASTRAS: Federación Nacional Sindical de Trabajadores Salvadoreños (National Union Federation of Salvadorean Workers).
8. UNTS: Unión Nacional de Trabajadores Salvadoreños (National Union of Salvadorean Workers).
9. Atilio: Commander Joaquín Villalobos, Secretary General of the Partido de la Revolución Salvadoreña (Salvadorean Revolutionary Party).
10. Colonel René Emilio Ponce, head of the Joint Chiefs of Staff.
11. In the 19th century an American named William Walker invaded Central America with a mercenary army, declaring himself President of Nicaragua before being forced out of the region.
12. Metrocentro is a large shopping centre in San Salvador.
13. UCA: Universidad Centroamericana José Simeón Cañas, San Salvador.
14. P. Ignacio Ellacuría, rector of the UCA.
15. Colonia Escalón is San Salvador's wealthiest neighbourhood.
16. Chico: Commander Claudio Rabindranath Armijo, member of the Political Commission of the PRS and of the Joint Chiefs of Staff of the Central Front."Modesto Ramírez."
17. General Maxwell Thurman: the ex-Chief of the US Southern Command, whose headquarters are in Panama.
18. General Humberto Larios: Minister of Defense.
19. Renatos: nickname for those belonging to the RN (Resistencia Nacional/National Resistance), one of the five political and military organizations that formed the FMLN.
20. Fernán Cienfuegos: leader of the Resistencia Nacional.

8

How to Make an Echo... of Moscow

Serguei Korzoun

If a year ago someone had told me that the most prominent personalities in the world of politics, diplomacy, the economy, science and culture, could be called upon to settle into our microscopic studios in the heart of Moscow, I would have laughed very hard. Such nice dreams — I wouldn't have believed them at all.

Today I don't laugh, because I'm well aware of its price. It's not measured in rubles or dollars, but in overworked days for our team of twenty-odd people, in sleepless nights spent reflecting long and hard on free radio broadcasting in our country, and in our small radio station in particular. How do you make an Echo of Moscow a free echo in a country which isn't, and among people who aren't?

The fame and the almost worldwide interest which Echo of Moscow is now enjoying, are no doubt connected to the events of August 1991, in Moscow. Events which some term the "coup d'état" or the *"putsch,"* others call the "revolution," while the third and largest group refer to it as the "continuation of the eternal mess." From August 19th to 21st 1991, Echo of Moscow, cut off from its transmitter four times, was the only radio station in Moscow to follow, broadcasting live, the vicissitudes of the "theatrical coup" which appears to have brought profound changes to our country, the former Soviet Union. I will come back to these three days after a small historical detour along the winding roads of independent radio in Moscow.

THE DEVELOPMENT OF INDEPENDENT RADIO IN MOSCOW

As I write these lines, there is no law regulating the distribution of broadcast frequencies for radio and television in the state of Russia. This law is foreseen for 1992. But in 1990 — the year when the idea for our radio station began to take shape — the Soviet State's domination of television and radio broadcasting was absolute.

The first swallows announcing the coming of spring for independent radio in the USSR came on April 30, 1990.

On this day, two radio stations appeared almost simultaneously on Moscow's airwaves — on frequencies granted by the all-powerful Gosteleradio (the USSR's State Committee for Radio and Television). The two stations were commercial music stations. Both had French backing and both, initially, were very dependent on State structures. Europa Plus is doing well today and expanding its programming. Nostalgia-Moscow recently had to redefine itself while collecting a second wind. Today, you can tune in to almost ten music stations in Moscow.

On August 1, 1990, a law regulating the press and other media came into effect. It said little about the broadcast media, and thus had the merit of not hampering radio's birth or development. On August 22, the first truly independent radio station began broadcasting. It was radio Echo of Moscow. The station would certainly never have been launched without the support of its sponsors. The newspaper *Ogonyok* provided the start-up funds; the Radio Association offered the medium-wave transmitter, antenna, frequency and transmission lines; the local municipality (the Soviet of Moscow) provided essential support and (mostly moral) assistance; and the Faculty of Journalism at Moscow University gave moral support as well as promises to provide help of all kinds. Once born, the child was thrown, without trumpets or fanfare, into the deep waters of political and financial insecurity. "Learn to swim on your own," the sponsors seemed to say. This could not have corresponded better with the most ardent wishes of the team as it settled itself into the studio furnished with rudimentary equipment. We had our work cut out for us, but what did it matter if, in the eyes of any radio professional, the equipment could have passed for museum pieces?

In a sense, all of Soviet radio and television could have been described as a museum in 1989, but a private museum belonging to the *apparatchiks.* Serguei Bountman and I had other ideas of what was possible. We had both worked at the French language service of Radio Moscow International for over ten years — a small part of the elephantesque Gosteleradio. Gorbachev-style perestroika had given us the opportunity to travel a bit, to go to France on several occasions and to get to know something of its radio landscape. I even had the chance to work at the Paris station, Kiss-FM, for twenty days, with a group of Soviet radio journalists. Understandably, we felt a bit confined upon our return. In our "museum" the release of each programme necessitated the signatures of a thousand directors. Their biggest concern was to avoid making a political faux-pas which would jeopardize their positions in the hierarchy of the Communist Party and the State. And the best way to avoid such faux-pas as we know very well, is to not do anything at all.

With other journalists, we tried to change things by proposing new programmes for Radio Moscow International. But the inertia of the State radio machine was such that, even in the throes of perestroika, anything new was engulfed in the never-ending sea of official commentary, called "bricks" in our professional jargon.

During this time I put a good deal of effort into finding ways to get a transmitter and a frequency, as well as funding for a station such as the one I conceived of, but until 1990 it was all in vain. Then in April 1990, luck smiled upon me. A friend proposed that I become Editor In Chief of a new radio station whose technical and financial bases seemed to be covered. I immediately arranged a meeting with the people responsible for this initiative. For the most part they were audio professionals who had no notion of radio programming. After talking to them, I accepted the offer without hesitation.

What did I lose? A more or less comfortable position, it's true, in a large State radio station with a highly developed, but inept, infrastructure. I lost almost all my social security, not altogether unimportant — believe me — in a country where the society is everything, and the individual, nothing. I also lost the few dozen francophone listeners who tuned into my programme. Should I have regretted it?

What would I find in this new venture? Well, I wasn't sure, but I supposed I would find freedom of action and of speech. And I did. The feeling of freedom began to dull a bit as the months went by, but I still remember the second day of broadcasting when I spoke simply, just like this, live on-air to people who simply wanted to phone in and say something to other listeners and myself. This was the first type of programming we broadcast. I felt myself flapping my wings. At first, listeners did not believe — didn't want to believe — that everything was happening live, even as they heard their own voices on their radio receivers. A few even went so far as to suppose that we were working for the KGB, and that our frank discussions were being taped for secret service files. Such were the first steps toward freedom as we tried, along with our listeners, to explore the vast expanse of possibilities that were offered to us.

Freedom — one gets used to it quickly. But as time goes by, the feeling of responsibility becomes heavier and heavier. Far from radically improving, the situation of the free media in Russia seemed to reverse itself. After a notable opening up, we observed more and more insistent measures to tighten the screws on the media whose publications and programmes did not correspond exactly with the expectations of the new power-holders. The authority of these power-holders in a newly sovereign Russia seemed to have replaced "the iron fist" of the old USSR. Power always seems to aspire to monopoly... And so in a situation where not everything that will affect the station is under your control, the responsibility that you feel towards the people who have followed you and your recalcitrant radio station is perhaps the hardest thing to bear.

What's needed to create a radio station? A transmitter, a microphone, a turntable, people who have something to say... The reality of radio in our country is much more complex. To begin operating a station, at least two thousand eight hundred and forty-eight agreements, from a thousand three-hundred and twenty-three organizations and institutions are needed. I'm not joking. Transmitters, for example, are not sold, but rather, "accorded" or "attributed," as are broadcast frequencies. And the designation of frequencies depends not on the application of the law but upon the good or bad will of the telecommunications officials. A cable link between the studio and transmitter isn't good enough for FM stereo broadcasting, but a hertzian hook-up isn't authorized in Moscow "for security reasons." Renting an office which will respond to the needs of a radio station is no small feat in Moscow, while using a State studio means risking being arbitrarily cut off from it at some point. This actually happened to us when Gosteleradio broke our contract without prior notice.

And I haven't even mentioned the question of funding yet. It's a matter of time, perhaps. In the beginning, the sponsors of Echo of Moscow provided start-up funds. This was a charitable gesture, a gesture of goodwill, of support for democracy, as we wouldn't really be able to depend on their money in the future. We have all the features of a free radio station, both politically and journalistically, but we finance ourselves like a commercial station. So we are fuelled by advertising, while the programming is non-commercial in nature. These last few months we've even made a small profit, so that we can develop without having to borrow.

We are aware of the ravages of advertising, but we still follow a general private radio model. The journalists hold 40% of the stocks in the station, with the rest belonging to the founding parties. The prestige we've won allows us to look to the future with optimism. We are strong enough and vigilant enough not to let ourselves be swallowed up by domestic or foreign capitalists. If the announced economic reforms go well and an advertising market is formed in Russia, we'll be in a good starting position. As for other funding sources, we foresee selling programmes to other stations and perhaps obtaining income through publications (our first book has just come out). Other financially viable activities are also planned, but that's up to the station's management. As journalists, we are first and foremost committed to refining our programming and not becoming simply a support mechanism for advertising.

Our original and eclectic programming reflects the wishes of the journalists at Echo of Moscow to compete with the national general radio in all areas, across all age groups. We're doing well according to the most recent poll of Moscow listeners, which gives us a loyal listenership of 7% (more than 12% among people in higher education), and 21% who listen to us periodically. The highest listenership is in the morning with up to three million listeners.

Politics, the economy, business, sports, culture, entertainment, commentary, readings and plays — in principle, all these subjects have the right to be broadcast at our station. But our main efforts are dedicated to the news. While news in the form of bulletins, reports and magazine programmes occupies only a tenth of our air time, its production occupies up to two-thirds of our staff. We have news agencies, special correspondents, stringers, and contact personnel in different spheres at our disposal in order to provide objective news coverage. This requires a lot of skill and money, but it's worth it in the long-run. The desire to be a quick and reliable source of information remains one of the greatest motivations for our journalists.

THE ECHO OF AN ARMED ATTACK

During the night of January 13, 1991, programme host Serguei Bountman was awakened by a phone call from a friend in Vilnius who told him that gunfire could be heard in the city. At the time we were broadcasting only three hours of programming a day, in the evenings. However, at a dawn meeting in our studio, having learned of the army and KGB attack on the Lithuanian radio and television building, we decided to hook up the transmitter well before normal broadcasting time.

We knew perfectly well that our voice would be the only echo of this armed attack. We were lucky enough to have two correspondents in Vilnius. It was a Sunday — and the daily newspapers don't publish Sundays or Mondays. And, as we expected, the State radio and television didn't breathe a word about the events. Without us, the coup would have passed unnoticed by the larger public. We were determined to speak out that day, from morning to night. And we were heard. Not only by our 300,000 daily listeners, but by some millions of Muscovites who were turning their radio dials searching for objective information.

We brandished our weapon of information and at the same time won the sympathies of Moscow's intelligentsia. Before these events, we had to explain at length what the station was about when we invited someone to participate in our programming. From January 13 on, it was enough to say "Echo of Moscow" in order to hear a "yes, of course." A "no" as well, at times, but much more rarely. A few days later, we expanded our programming to eight hours a day, and continued at this pace, all the while awaiting an order of technical equipment which would permit us to broadcast 24 hours a day.

AUGUST 1991

Given our reputation it was no surprise that Echo of Moscow was the first medium to be closed down on the day of the attempted coup d'état in Moscow, on August 19, 1991.

On that morning, at 6:20 a.m., I entered the building which houses our offices and studio, located a few steps away from the Kremlin. I was replacing a programme host who was ill. It was only then that I heard the national radio announce President Gorbachev's illness and the introduction of emergency measures "in some regions of the country." My first thought was: "This time, they will certainly silence us, the lesson of Vilnius must have been learned." I was slightly wrong, for two minutes later the transmitter technicians assured me that we'd be on-air at 7:00 a.m., as usual. My second thought was: "What are they stirring up? This coup d'état will be the *coup-de-grace* of Communism in the USSR, for it will never succeed!" Here I was correct. My third thought was that all the programming initially planned for the day would have to be cancelled — nothing was accurate anymore. It would all have to be replaced.

After alerting our whole team, I telephoned a few people who would be capable of analyzing the situation on-air. I selected a few Soviet "social" rock songs as support music, valuable not so much for their music as for their anti-totalitarian lyrics.

At exactly 7:00 I took my seat in front of the console and the microphone, and my first few words went something like, "It's a bad morning today. If you've just woken up, we'll tell you why." We broadcast official information as well as dispatches from our correspondents about the movement of troops throughout the city. I awaited the arrival of my guests and, at 7:45, a group of people appeared in the studio. The face of one of them seemed very familiar to me and, taking advantage of a musical break, I rose to shake their hands and invite them to take a seat in front of the mike. A few seconds later, I realized that the familiar face belonged to one of the higher-ups at the telecommunications service (whose offices are just next door). The others introduced themselves as officers of the KGB!

— "Is this the place where the programme is being done?" one of them asked me.
— "Yes, this is it, strange as it may seem," I replied, taking a look around me — our decrepit equipment could have led anyone to believe they were mistaken.
— "You must cease broadcasting."
— "Why?"
— "The Emergency Measures — you know."
— "Show me the papers that entitle you to close us down."
— "But you know that with the announcement of Emergency Measures all the media must go under control."
— "Wait," I replied, reading from a copy of the official text, "it states that the Emergency Measures are being introduced in certain regions. The city of Moscow isn't mentioned here."
— "But that goes without saying. You must terminate."
— "No, I can't do that. In the absence of the appropriate papers I'll do nothing of the sort."

The KGB man continued to insist, but without doing anything to stop the show there in the studio. His team — five or six people, all of slight build and in civilian dress did not have the appearance of a commando. I was already thinking that despite any dispute, I was going to continue the program, and was ready to hand the mike over to my real guest who had just arrived. Just then one of our journalists entered and told us that the control receiver was dead — the radio signal was not being transmitted any longer. I looked at my watch — it was two minutes to 8:00.

They had stopped us by disconnecting the studio from the transmitter. The programme was cut off. But the real work was just beginning. Probably having judged their task accomplished, the KGB men disappeared without a trace, but the technicians upon whom the connection depended flatly refused to reconnect us to the transmitter, claiming that it was a technical failure. Still, the departure of the KGB men left us room to manoeuvre and the hope of reconnecting later.

We had three exhausting days of work ahead of us. Exhausting, but in many ways very easy and fruitful. The fact is that none of the channels of information were cut by the army: the telephones didn't stop ringing, the fax emitted an uninterrupted stream, all the agencies did their best to function under an emergency regime. A real bargain for the journalists! Cut off from our antenna on the first day, we ourselves functioned as a press agency by retransmitting news digests to other media, including foreign stations, notably the BBC and Radio Liberty. At the same time we waged a real fight for our own airwaves. On the second day of the coup — August 20 — we succeeded in reinstating our programming thanks to the support of a team of technicians. It was at 1:40 p.m., and I remember this moment very well, as I had never before been moved by such a rush of forces. I hosted the programmes that day and the first three hours went by without a hitch. Agency information, music, live phone calls from the Russian Parliament which was barricaded and under siege, guests in studio — all of these followed one another at a crazy pace. Our listeners telephoned us as well and brought us cake, coffee and cigarettes to help us hold our ground.

That evening, on the televised news, we learned some significant official information — a decree of the coup leaders imposed the closure of several media outlets. Echo of Moscow was mentioned as "the radio station which is not contributing to stabilizing the situation." We would have liked to carry another of their attempts to close us down live but this time our transmitter was disconnected . We mobilized all our friends and managed to reconnect one hour later. The third disconnection hit us at 1:00 a.m. — during the tensest moment of the coup. We had at least had the time to inform our listeners of the first blood shed in the streets of Moscow.

The news of the violence, and being closed down at such a crucial moment, left us disheartened. In addition, we knew from information continuing to reach us that things were not going well in the vicinity of the Russian parliament, and that a direct attack was being prepared. What's more, an unknown radio station using the name Echo of Moscow was broadcasting misinformation on our airwaves! In that night's disorder, we didn't take the time to tape their programmes. But there was no doubt that it was a "radio game" of the secret service who were controlling the assault. The question of *who* did it remains officially unanswered. The KGB replied to all the other questions of the inquiry commission, but not that one. And any hope of ever getting an answer has been dampened by the reorganization of the secret service.

At around 3:00 a.m. we received a call from a supporter within the Ministry of Telecommunications asking us if we were ready to begin broadcasting again. My response was, "yes, of course." And so technicians arranged to connect our little studio to a transmitter located ten kilometres away, via a simple telephone line. It worked! It worked so well that the coup leaders were stumped. How could a disconnected station continue to broadcast? They resorted to sending a KGB commando to destroy the transmitter and finish us off once and for all. But it was already August 21, and a few hours later the defeat of the coup was evident to everyone. On their own initiative the technicians reconnected everything they could, including a back-up transmitter.

In the same remarkable spirit, soldiers from a detachment outside Moscow, having discovered that our transmitter was silent, loaded a similar one onto a truck, with the intention of bringing it to us! They were already heading our way when they heard our signal start up and turned back. Hats off!

A month later the journalists who came to interview us were more numerous than those in our editorial room. Falling down from fatigue, tired of answering the same questions, we never turned any of them away. The publicity was a chance to become known around the world. Not too bad for a "commercial" station that's as poor as a mouse.

FUTURE ECHOES

We now know that the future of Echo of Moscow is in the hands of its journalists, and we are delighted. It is clear that we can operate as a commercial station without abandoning our journalistic ideals. In the post-coup period the monopoly of the USSR State Radio-Television, along with the Soviet Union itself, disappeared completely. But a new monopoly is trying to take root — the Russian State Radio-Television. It hoards the best frequencies, the most powerful transmitters, and uses advertising to the fullest in order to inflate journalists' salaries. In short, a perfidious competition is unfolding and the State has the position of advantage. At the same time, private music stations, often created through State participation, are growing like mushrooms, making full use of the facilities offered by the high authorities. For the moment, Echo of Moscow is holding its ground. The latest poll placed us second in all of Moscow, just behind Europa Plus. The other stations are lagging far behind.

Because we were avoiding the involvement of large entrepreneurs, we lost a bit of time in reequipping ourselves. In the end, we were able to obtain a well-equipped studio with the help of the American foundation, Soros. So we will have one less problem. With the consent of the original funders we have adopted a policy of investing 40% of revenue in news production. The financing of the station is ensured by advertising which, since the coup, has brought in one million rubles a month. The ruble isn't a strong currency however. Its freefall worries us and we're pinning our hopes on the economic reforms instituted in Russia.

One of our greatest advantages is that none of the new radio stations has dared to challenge us on our territory — the area of serious news. We have a huge network of correspondents, contacts throughout the country and in the old republics of the USSR, and we are beginning to build an international network. In effect we have a monopoly in Moscow because the State radio, though better equipped, doesn't take as much care with the speed or format of its news programming. While this position threatens to spoil us, we are determined not to succumb to the temptation of loosening up, even a bit.

The future won't be easy for us, we know. The new authorities see us more and more in a negative light. But none of this prevents us from gathering into our studios all types of minorities, from having a good time when we want to, and from cursing between our teeth as we kick our broken old equipment while presenting a calm front to our listeners.

We keep going with the Echo of Moscow, which is more than a passion — it's a veritable drug. But not one that kills. One that reinvigorates, that stimulates us and drives us forward, crazy people that we are. Only a crazy person could believe in making an Echo... of Moscow.

* * *

9

A New Dawn for Freedom of Speech : Radio Soleil

Joseph Georges with assistance from Isabelle Fortin

In 1978, Haiti was still suffering under the dictatorship of Jean Claude Duvalier. Repression was rampant and any opposition to the regime was immediately squashed. Duvalier, who had replaced his father as president a few years earlier, was later to declare himself President-for-life. International pressure had forced the government to permit a certain opening and a few radio stations and newspapers were attempting to report on the repression.

At the same time, the Catholic Church was re-examining its role in Latin America. At a conference in Medellin, Colombia, Catholic Bishops spoke of the need for the Church to become involved in the struggles of the people of Latin American and the Caribbean and of the importance of the media in combatting political repression.

It was in this context that the Episcopalian Conference of Haiti created Radio Soleil (Sun Radio) to work alongside the people against repression and for the promotion of human rights.

RADIO SOLEIL AND THE DICTATORSHIP

Radio Soleil's first confrontation with the dictatorship came in 1980 when the government arrested journalists from Radio Haiti Inter, a commercial station that often took progressive political positions. These journalists had begun broadcasting news in Creole[1] that was critical of the Duvalier regime, and the station director, Jean Dominique, and some staff were forced into exile. Expressing our solidarity with the journalists, Radio

Soleil protested the events as yet another abuse of human rights and another reason to keep working for an end to the dictatorship. At a time when people were feeling that they had suffered another defeat, Radio Soleil encouraged them not to despair.

Radio Soleil was again at the forefront of the resistance with its role in the release of Gérard Duclerville, a Catholic activist who was detained by the government in 1982. The authorities denied they were holding Duclerville. However, Radio Soleil persisted with daily reports about the detention, saying each time: Today, November 17, Gérard Duclerville, arrested on such-and-such a day was not released. Today, November 18, Gérard Duclerville, arrested on such-and-such a day was not released. We kept this up until his release in February, 1983. The campaign to release Duclerville was the catalyst for the creation of a nationwide solidarity network, the first time that students, teachers, priests, and representatives of neighbourhood and peasant organisations worked together. By the end of the campaign the Episcopalian Council had made Duclerville's release a precondition for Pope John Paul's planned visit in March.

The papal visit provided us with yet another opportunity to speak out against the dictatorship. "Something must change in Haiti," pronounced Pope John Paul II at the Port au Prince Cathedral. For the next five years this statement became a theme for Radio Soleil, as we tried to identify the "something" that had to change. Our programmes addressed issues of justice, and the lack of it. We talked about the enormous privileges of the land-owning class, such as the right to go to school. We spoke of the lack of decent health services and of the Tontons Macoutes.[2] Each time a government official claimed the regime was democratic, we pointed to the facts that contradicted the claim.

GARANTI LA LOI

These early experiences revealed the power of radio to those of us at Radio Soleil, and to the rest of the Haitian people. However, it was not until 1985, when President Duvalier announced that there would be a referendum in which people would be able to choose between one form of dictatorship or another, that we began to use this power to its full potential. We responded to the referendum with a series of skits — one of our most effective and popular campaigns ever. The airing of the first skit caused an uproar across the country and got everyone tuning in. Listeners asked to have it rebroadcast, which we did, three times a day. The programme was called *Garanti la loi* (Uphold the Law). The regular cast included two peasants (a man and a woman), a few peasant youths, and a *griot* (an experienced elder). These people met each morning under a tree and discussed their problems. The peasant man always started out by saying he was hungry and couldn't find anything to eat; that he had been to the hospital and there was no medicine; and that the dispensary was far away and it took him a long time to get there. One day he told about how he had met another peasant on the road who told him something was about to happen in the country. The first man asked:

— "But what is going to happen?," and the second replied:
— "Aren't you aware of the referendum?"

The first man did not understand what this was about,

— "What are they referring too? And who is dumb?" he said.

We did a lot of scenes that made fun of the terminology of the referendum. In the end, the peasant never understood what it meant. An opportunity to choose between one form of President-for-life and another didn't make much sense.

The peasant women asked questions about democracy:

> "Will it come in a plane?," she asked. She looked in sky and didn't see anything. Then she looked on the ground and didn't see anything, either. Democracy was nowhere to be found in Haiti. We ridiculed the government's entire political philosophy. One day, the *griot* talked about the constitution and everyone was stunned.

"What does the constitution mean? Does such a thing exist? I didn't realize that there was a constitution and that the president's name was in it as president-for-life!"

The peasant man asked if it was normal for the president's name to appear in the constitution. The *griot* said that it was not. There was also a stranger among them, a *mon blanc* (a friendly term for a white foreigner) who described and explained experiences in other countries, pointing out to people that Haiti's political situation wasn't normal.

THE STATE'S REACTION

One day the Ministers of the Interior, External Affairs, and Information called the station director in. The Minister of External Affairs said to him, "Director, I listen to your skits every morning, they're really fantastic, and very interesting. I'd like to participate. Could I possibly give you a cassette?"

The Minister gave us a cassette, and asked that it be included in our show. Later we met to discuss what to do with it. We decided to start the skit, as usual, with the peasant man. He stated that in his region there were no cars or ambulances, while in Port-au-Prince he had seen several cars in the Ministries' courtyards. The cars were equipped with loudspeakers that made noise and spread propaganda. This was just the sort of naive but insightful criticism a peasant would make. At this point one of the youths in the skit turned on his radio and invited the others to listen to what appeared to be a government announcement. Everyone listened, and we then played the government's cassette. The characters in the skit criticized what they heard on the radio, pointing out the contradictions. A few days after we aired the show, the authorities cut the electricity and telephone, and jammed the station's signal.

Fortunately, our technician succeeded in thwarting the jamming and we managed to get electricity from a neighbour so we were able to continue our work and keep broadcasting *Garanti la Loi* three times a day. We received hundreds of letters from the provinces, with people's opinions on the referendum. They were all against it.

On referendum day, we broadcast reports from clandestine correspondents. They were located at various polling sites and by identifying license plates, they were able to follow buses that left working-class neighbourhoods, packed with voters paid by the government. These buses went from polling station to polling station, and people voted several times. We secretly recorded their accounts:

— "I voted twenty times. I voted one-hundred times."
— "Why did you vote 'yes'?"
— "I didn't choose. I was given a ballot already marked 'yes'."

In other areas people came down from the mountains to vote and discovered the ballot boxes already full. Through our correspondents, we were able to record their accounts, too. All over the country those who went to vote were paid to do so, and we had recordings to prove it:

— "Dérélus, give me my dollar, I already voted!"

When the government realized that everyone knew the referendum was a fraud, and that we were broadcasting the news, they shut the station. We were linked by phone to two other stations in the provinces and so for a while our programmes were still heard outside Port-au-Prince, but they soon found this out and cut the phone lines. Undefeated, we sent the cassettes to the other stations by bus every day.

On the day of the referendum we were told by supporters in the neighbourhood that the station director had been arrested and hit by soldiers and that he was to be deported the same day.[3] We immediately took steps to get the embassies and the Church to intervene and prevent the expulsion. The director was released later that day and we produced a special edition of *Garanti la loi*. In it the peasant hit the *mon blanc* (who was played by the director) in the same way as the soldiers had. The *mon blanc* cried out and told the story of what had happened to him that day, but in a comical fashion. Then the peasant boasted that, for the first time in his life he had been able to ride in an air-conditioned bus, that he had voted 100 times, and that he had even been paid for it. Two days later the director was deported.

THE PRESSURE INCREASES

From November 1985 to December 1985, fifteen upper level government officials, including four ministers of state, paid us visits. On their final visit, they told us, "We now own Radio Soleil. You will follow our orders. In this battle you will lose because we have the weapons and the Church has none."

Each time we received this type of visit we informed our listeners on air. This irritated the ministers. The day of their final visit we once again broadcast the news. This time however, we received calls from Church officials asking us to stop because they had received threats from the authorities. We no longer had the right to broadcast news, but we continued to play political music. This angered the authorities just as much, and they threatened to issue a decree banning music containing protest messages. On December 4, the army showed up and broke equipment at the transmitter site and at the station, forcing us off the air.

On the same day I returned to the station from a trip abroad. When I arrived the soldiers told me that the army now owned the station and that I could not stay. They searched my suitcase and found some Catholic newspapers. I told them that the information was harmless, but they replied that it came from Canada and Yugoslavia. "Jean-Claude doesn't have relations with those countries. They're communist countries! You are under arrest!"

Later, after eating, the soldiers said I seemed like an okay type and could return to the station if I wanted to. We were able to go back to work, even though the station was off the air. For the next while we fed the soldiers three times a day and they watched T.V. and didn't bother keeping watch on the station.

In the final days of December 1985, popular and international pressure called for Radio Soleil to be reopened. At one point John Littleton, a religious singer, was in Haiti on a concert tour. At every concert the announcer thanked the various radio stations for their help in promoting the concert. Each time he got to Radio Soleil, which he thanked even though we were not on the air, there was a standing ovation. The last performance on Littleton's tour was a benefit for a youth organisation. When the show was over the people spilled into the streets in a spontaneous demonstration, demanding that Radio Soleil be reopened.

After that, things changed quickly. The situation was so tense that the government actually started putting pressure on us to reopen the station. Finally, on December 24, in the middle of the night, we found ourselves at the transmitter site supervising government technicians while they repaired the damage they had caused. We went on the air again on December 31, with the same content, assuring our listeners that we had not changed and that we would not.

THE DAYS LEADING UP TO FEBRUARY 7, 1986

Our first programme when we went back on the air was a live broadcast of an open-air mass. We wanted to take some time before starting to broadcast news programmes again, but public pressure soon got them back on the air. As soon as we started, the government started harassing us again. It was very tense. On the one hand, we were receiving phone calls threatening to throw grenades at us, and on the other, calls from people telling us they were going to form security brigades to protect us.

The situation was heating up and by early January the repression was very intense and people were becoming discouraged. We launched a show called *Seven Diocese in Seven Days*. The show's host travelled to each community and talked with the locals about the situation in Haiti. They discussed how it was unjust and unacceptable and how it was against the teachings of Jesus Christ. The programme went into people's homes with reassurance and encouragement. The essential message was, "Hello, how are you? We know you have lost parents, brothers, sisters or children and that these are hard times. But we have come to tell you not to despair, that there are still ways to fight."

Our plan was to close the show with simultaneous ecumenical services across the country. Protestants would visit Catholic communities, and vice versa. The services were supposed to end in demonstrations against the regime. However, the government felt so threatened that it called a meeting with the bishops to tell them to stop the programme. We refused to stop, despite the bishops' interference. On the seventh day, the demonstrations took place as we had planned. On January 31, the station was, once again, closed by the government. But this time, the closure was too late.

ONÈ! RÈSPÈ!

The demonstrations continued after January 31 and one week later, on February 7, President-for-life Jean Claude Duvalier left the country for good, creating new potential for democracy in Haiti.

Some people maintained that the struggle was over and that Radio Soleil's programming should become purely religious. The station staff didn't agree. On the contrary, we felt that this was precisely the moment to be with the people in drawing up a new blueprint for our society. Part of our contribution to this was the launching of a new programme, *Onè! Rèspè!* (Honour! Respect!), as a sequel to *Garanti la Loi*.

The programme was produced by the same team and had the same cross section of Haitian characters, all with different experiences and different levels of education. One day we discussed health, another repression, and so on for the whole week. The programme started with a traditional peasant greeting, *"Onè! Rèspè!,"* to address the families participating in the project.

Members of the community sent letters which we read at the beginning of the programme. These letters included thoughts on problems encountered by families in the various regions. They also asked that we come and visit them. So we took the show to the regions. We were always very warmly received and there was remarkable contact and familiarity between the people and ourselves. At times people worked as journalists themselves, putting their own reports on cassettes and sending them to us for broadcast. They also sent poems, songs and political pieces. They were preparing themselves for times of conflict. They even sent us practical information, like how to preserve mangoes. The programme was part of a conscious effort to show the worth of peasants' work, both social and cultural.

Although Duvalier was gone, there was still a lot of repression. One of the things we did to encourage people was organise a song contest in which we invited people to sing about their problems. The group that won had written a song against increasing contraband that was destroying rice production in Artibonite (an irrigated rice-producing region in the centre of the country). They also sang songs about a massacre of 600 peasants in Jean Rabel (a town in the northwest region of the country). These songs were performed with traditional instruments.

One of our principal themes, adopted as well by several peasant organisations, was "Organisation or Death!." We provided techniques for organizing that were not simply based on experts' know-how, but on the basis of successful experiences throughout the country. The show was considered enemy number one for several successive governments - Namphy, Manigat, Avril and the others. It continued until 1989, when the pressure from conservative elements in the Church forced the firing of the production team.

NOVEMBER, 1987

With Duvalier gone, the country could work toward its first democratic elections. An election was called for November, 1987 but in the end there was too much violence and it had to be postponed. It soon became clear the transition would not be an easy one. The repression continued. In one instance a teacher from a literacy project was detained by the army. (To this day we do not know if he was killed). We did a programme in solidarity with the teacher which included a skit in which his new-born baby asked where her father was. On November 7, there was a national demonstration and almost 300,000 people gathered in the capital to say no to the Macoutes, their endless killing and their muzzling of Radio Soleil. There was supposed to be a march, starting at the station and ending at a small church. The army started a rumour that the people at the station had assassinated someone. When the procession prepared to leave, the army started shooting at the crowd and the station. We spent three hours lying on the ground to avoid the gunshots, lightbulbs exploding over our heads. Each time people reported to police that we were being shot at, they would deny it, saying that in fact we were the ones shooting at the army.

On November 28, foreign journalists and correspondents held a press conference at Radio Soleil denouncing the fact the army would not allow them travel to the countryside to report on the elections. We broadcast it live. At 9:00 that evening we received two anonymous calls warning us to leave the station because we were going to be bombed. We took our time and finished our work. We had just left the station when the shooting started. The transmitter had already been set on fire by the time the station was attacked by three trucks, machine guns and grenades. Eighteen people were wounded and one was killed in the fire.

We took stock of the damage the next day: the technician and guard's houses and several cars had been burned. The ten kilowatt transmitter was damaged but luckily only the outside had burned. Using a 1 kilowatt backup transmitter, we were back at work within two days, reassuring the public with the same energy as before. We received an impressive showing of solidarity and within one month we had raised $90,000 to buy another 10 kilowatt transmitter. The money came from both national and international sources and it came in so quickly that we actually had to tell people to stop sending money. People walked kilometres to bring us two gourds (the local currency), others $20. In Port-au-Prince alone we raised $20,000. That year we received the Letellier-Moffit award, in recognition of our work in popular and alternative communication and for our work in promoting respect for human rights with, among others, our show *Onè! Rèspè!* Even this caused us problems because the award came from a so-called socialist organization.

CONCLUSION

If the "Sun" succeeded in bringing a few rays of freedom, it is due to a particular vision of struggle, which can be summarized in the simple strategy we employed, especially in difficult moments: Protect yourself and attack. This strategy required that a philosophy of struggle pervade all aspects of the station's programming: news, educational, religious and music shows. As such, everything we broadcast was grounded in our commitment to political and social change. Listener participation was our other essential tool, because it was not only the station staff that was committed to change, but also and especially the listeners. It was their participation that drove Radio Soleil and enabled it to make a difference. An example: Elifet is in Port-au-Prince and has been attacked by the Tontons Macoutes. Fidelia is from Carrefour and her mother is in prison. In these two towns fear has gripped the people. But Elifet turns on his radio and hears Ekzius denouncing the repression of the people in his area, Bochan, in the north-west. In Petit-Goave, Adelaide demands the release of her father. Elifet and Fidelia, having been completely discouraged, hear these two messages and find new courage. They head off to the station to make their denunciations as well.

The staff's militancy played an instrumental role in helping the people overcome their fear. The people's own analysis of the state of affairs helped the station's work. People came up with their own ideas about how their living conditions could be changed. This constant will to overcome fear encouraged us to take on nation-wide initiatives, that on several occasions succeeded in changing attitudes among the people and within the government.

Our best shows were produced spontaneously and creatively. They were used to circumvent the repression, to protect ourselves and to protect the people. The names of those who gave testimonies were never revealed. The characters in the socio-dramas were often invented. At Radio Soleil, it was the listeners who had the real radio power. Many came to sleep at the station, to protect what they saw as their own radio. They brought food for the staff, searched for news, even the most confidential, to give to the journalists. Our programmes, in turn, protected the listeners, discreetly or directly.

POSTSCRIPT: A CHANGE OF COURSE

We continued to do our work, trying to contribute to the building of a new society in Haiti, until 1989 when conservative and orthodox elements within the Church managed to gain sway in the Episcopalian Conference and ordered the radio station to change course. Most of the programming staff was fired.

Since the coup d'état on September 29, 1991, which overthrew the first democratically elected government in Haiti, Radio Soleil has become a propaganda tool for the dictators. This affected the former staff because, siding as we did with the listeners, we no longer could depend on the station's support, or on its previously unquestionable concern for the truth. In contrast to the courage which it had shown in the past, the station no longer gave a voice to the suffering and fear of a threatened people. Radio Soleil did not denounce the aggression, intimidation and elimination of journalists and correspondents, or the gagging of the press. It did not denounce the systematic repression of peasant and popular organisations. Instead it kept silent, handing over the microphone to the assassins who mocked the people's faith in truth and justice.

Among ourselves, the members of the old team, we shared our pain and waited in vain for changes in programming. Finally we understood both what it meant to be a listener, and what listeners of a liberation radio hoped for.

* * *

NOTES

1. Although Creole is the daily language of Haitians, most radio stations chose to broadcast in French, a language mastered by only a small elite. This policy had the effect of excluding the voices of most Haitians from radio.
2. The Tontons Macoutes were a private militia established by Duvalier.
3. At the time, the station director was a Belgian priest.

10

Zoom Black Magic Liberation Radio : The birth of the micro-radio movement in the USA

Ron Sakolsky

In the United States, in response to the government carrot of licensing status and the stick of anti-piracy crackdowns, many once adventurous community radio broadcasters have toned down their oppositional elements and have consciously or unconsciously become engaged in a process of self-censorship. One sign pointing in a different direction is the micro-radio movement, originating not on a college campus or in a university-based community, but in the heart of the black ghetto. This is the story of one micro-radio station, WTRA/Zoom Black Magic Liberation Radio in Springfield, Illinois.

The story unfolds at the John Hay Homes, a sprawling, low income public housing project located in Springfield's east side. It is a housing project that is almost exclusively African-American. Located just a short distance from the enshrined home of Abraham Lincoln, it's a part of Springfield that isn't on the tourist map. During the mid-eighties, the John Hay Tenants Rights Association (TRA) was formed to do issue-based, neighbourhood organizing.

Focusing first on expressway expansion and related school traffic safety issues, the TRA moved on to the issues of school bussing and the inadequate representation of the east side community under the archaic, commission form of government. Calling for more community control, they successfully challenged the local black bourgeoisie who claimed to represent them in a historic voting rights lawsuit, which resulted in the commission system being replaced with an aldermanic one.

The TRA then opposed an ordinance sponsored by their newly-elected black alderman which involved the purchase of scab coal from a Shell-owned mine which violated the boycott on Shell in response to its South African holdings. They also politically skewered the alderman's plan for a weak-kneed civilian review board for the police, proposing instead a much stronger one modeled on that of Berkeley, California.

Angered and dismayed by biased media coverage of these actions and its organizing campaigns, the TRA, in 1986, hit upon the idea of a community-based radio station to represent its point of view directly to its constituency and to communicate more effectively with a community which has an oral tradition and a high rate of functional illiteracy.

This idea was not unusual in itself. For example, ACORN (the Association of Community Organizations for Reform Now) had been using radio as an organizing tool for some time. However, the ACORN vision was more centralized in focus, more closely tied to coordinating national ACORN organizing goals among the local chapters, promoted relatively high wattage for maximum outreach, and was strictly legal.

In contrast, WTRA (as the station was originally named) was based on a decentralized model, had a symbiotic relationship with its community with no official membership base and no national ties. Disdaining professional trappings, it broadcast with low power and was not only illegal in the eyes of the Federal Communications Commission (FCC),[1] but defiantly so. Because of Springfield's apartheid housing patterns, it was clear that even a station of less than a watt with a radius of between one and two miles could cover 70% of the African-American community, the prime audience which the station desired to reach. Since it was not a clandestine station, it would, by its very openness, challenge the power of the federal government.

Given the TRA's non-compliance with FCC rules and regulations, though it continued to be involved in more mainstream community organizing activities, its primary funding agent, the Campaign for Human Development, cancelled its grant. Fortunately, before cancellation, $600 in grant money had already been spent to purchase the equipment necessary to set up the radio station. All that remained was to find an empty spot on the dial and start broadcasting.

The FCC model for radio broadcasters is based on scarcity. Asserting that the electromagnetic spectrum is finite, the FCC benignly agrees to act as the impartial gatekeeper for access to the airwaves in the name of the public interest. However, another explanation of federal radio communications policy might start with a question recently posed by M'banna Kantako, founder of the TRA and "deprogramming" director of the radio station since it has been on the air: "Why is it that in this country you can buy a fully assembled AK-47 easier than a radio transmitter?"

M'banna Kantako has been intrinsically linked to the evolution of the radio station from its inception as WTRA, into Zoom Black Magic Liberation Radio, and, most recently, into Black Liberation Radio. It is from his apartment at the John Hay Homes that the station transmits, and his living room is a gathering place for political activists, neighbours and friends to discuss the issues of the day. It is a focal point for community animation in which grievances are aired and aspirations articulated around the radio transmitter.

His name wasn't always Kantako. Born DeWayne Readus he later discarded it as a slave name, choosing for himself the name M'banna Kantako, symbolizing refusal, resistance, rebellion and a connection with Africa. According to Kantako:

> We were on the air 3 years before the FCC bust. It was just a party thing, and we partied because we didn't know that we were being wiped out. Once we got hip to it and started to identify those things that are used to wipe us out, like the police, then we became a threat to the government, and then, of course, they used another apparatus, the FCC, to declare us illegal.

Just before the cease and desist order was issued, Kantako, who was himself blinded as a young man in a beating at the hands of the police, had broadcast a series of shows which involved community people calling in and giving personal testimony about police brutality, or as Kantako calls it, "official government-sponsored terrorism." Springfield Police Chief Mike Walton quickly complained about the illegality of the station to the FCC, and in April of 1989, the officials knocked on Kantako's door demanding that he stop broadcasting or face a fine of $750 ($150 more than the cost of the station's equipment), pursuant to Section 301 of the Communications Act of 1934, for being an unlicensed station. Shutting down the station for a little less than 2 weeks to reflect on the situation, Kantako recalled from history that during slavery there had been laws against the slaves communicating with one another.

Bringing that history up to date, as Kantako told Rich Sherekis of the Illinois Times back in January of 1990, "We weren't around when they made those laws about licensing...We were sitting in the back of the bus somewhere. So why should we be responsible to obey laws that oppress us?" Furthermore, as he pointed out later that month at a conference on radio censorship held in Chicago, those laws are selectively enforced.

> If you are saying, "Don't give a damn about nobody. Get you a house. Get you a dog. Get you a swimming pool, and the hell with everybody else," then they will not only leave you on the air, they'll give you a bigger transmitter! But if you start talking about people coming together to fight against the system that's oppressing all of humanity, all across the planet, then they will find you. There is nowhere you can hide.

So, he decided to go back on the air as an open act of civil disobedience, risking confiscation of his equipment, FCC-imposed fines that could go as high as $10,000, and criminal penalties of as much as $100,000 and one year in prison. WTRA was not simply resuming operations, but consciously challenging the exclusion of low income people, particularly African-Americans, from the airwaves and offering an affordable alternative. In 1978 the FCC adopted a policy to give licenses only to stations broadcasting with 100 watts or more, replacing the old minimum standard of 10 watts. Start up costs for such a station run around $50,000 (including equipment costs, engineering surveys, legal fees and proving to the FCC that you're solvent.) The cost of meeting FCC requirements effectively silences many potential radio voices. As Kantako put it, "It's kind of like those black tie dinners at $25,000 a plate. You can come, if you've got $25,000. Anything you need to survive, they put a price tag on, and if you don't have it, you don't survive. They call our broadcasting controversial. We call it survival material."

Such survival material includes broadcasting local police communications live from the police scanner he has set up in his apartment. In a more humorous vein, the station once recorded the oinking and squealing of pigs in a central Illinois barnyard and broadcast it later, for a full 90 minutes, as a "secretly-recorded meeting at the Springfield police station."

While he likes a joke at the expense of the police, when he flipped the switch to go back on the air, Kantako was very serious about his historical mission. "Somebody tell the children how WTRA served as an advocate for the people when the police wouldn't police themselves...Somebody tell the people how we fought police brutality by broadcasting the personal testimonies of African-American victims." While he was not arrested, the FCC made clear to him that he was in violation of the code.

The only exemption to the FCC's licensing requirement is for extremely low power transmissions that can be heard no more than 25 yards away. So, unless it increased its wattage 100 fold, the station would not qualify for an FCC license. However, as Kantako has noted in expressing his contempt for the FCC licensing process, "Anything the government gives you, they can take away." He calls the FCC the "thought patrol." As he explains, "It's not legal in this country for people to do anything to empower themselves, and in particular the black community. Don't no government give you freedom of speech. Don't no government own the air."

Ironically, the Objectives of the FCC Commissioners, as listed in the 1990 budget, call for the Commission "to eliminate government actions that infringe upon the freedom of speech and the press." Kantako is calling their bluff by demanding that the government pay more than just lip service to the constitutional guarantees of free speech and equal protection under the law. In terms of the latter, while blacks compose 12% of the nation's population, they only own 2% of its radio stations for an exclusion rate of 600%, dramatically higher if class and gender are brought into the picture. Providing equal protection, by waiving license requirements or by setting up a separate category for low power community broadcasting licenses, is a political choice the FCC seems unwilling to offer, despite the Federal Communications Act's call for "fair, efficient and equitable" distribution of radio services.

The types of voices heard on WTRA when it started and those heard on Black Liberation Radio today have changed somewhat over the years. The local authorities are one of the causes of this change. In the early days, most of the station's programmers were youth, learning radio skills and doing live hip hop mixes on the air, laying down the black liberation sound track of the Nineties. But there has been a constant barrage of police harassment directed at anyone involved with the station and more than a dozen of the young people on the air at the beginning have been expelled from school for, as Kantako puts it "anything from reading books on Malcolm X to not wanting to eat the red meat." In spite of the harassment, there are still youth involved with the station, but they come and go. Moreover, in addition to radio, many youth continue to be involved in the TRA's Marcus Garvey Freedom Summer School and the Malcolm X Library.

One of the things that has helped the station continue in the face of threats from local authorities and the FCC is the degree of national and international support it has gained. It has a high national profile with favourable articles appearing in a range of publications from the progressive press to the underground "'zines," news stories on NPR and MTV, a potential constitutional court case ("Black Liberation Radio vs. the FCC") presently being researched by the National Lawyers Guild, and international support from the World Association of Community Broadcasters (AMARC), along with articles appearing in the Italian and German press.

Yet all this publicity could not protect the station were it not for the strength of its grassroots community support. Kantako is not some outside agitator, but a lifelong resident of the community in which the station is situated. "I love to brag about the community I live in" he says. "This is a group of people that society has no need for and instead of laying down and dying, they've said, "let's arm ourselves with the necessary knowledge and we'll make a place for ourselves." If those in charge of the money won't include us, then we'll include ourselves." Going full circle, it is this kind of spirited resistance that, in turn, generated the national and international support in the first place, and that continues to do so. One of the results of this local, national and international alliance was a successful letter writing campaign that beat back a 1990 attempt to have the station evicted from its base in the John Hay Homes.

By 1991 the station had changed its name from WTRA to Black Liberation Radio, a change that was motivated by the desire to dissociate itself from official labelling devices and proclaim its right to exist without government sanction.

In addition to the immediate concerns of the local community, Black Liberation Radio's programming also deals with world issues in the same openly-oppositional way. During the recent war in the Middle East, Black Liberation Radio was the only station in Springfield that offered a position vigorously critical of the U.S. government, with both the commercial stations and the local university-based NPR[2] station busily involved in collaborating with the process of manufacturing consent. As Kantako has said:

> If anything, what people should have got out of the Persian Gulf massacre is how tightly the media is controlled by the military in-

> dustrial complex...Your station will get community support if you start telling the people the truth because all over the planet folks are dying to hear the truth and one way this multinational conglomerate has stayed in charge is by purposely making the people ignorant.

In addition to news and commentary, Black Liberation Radio has a music policy that offers a "yard-to-yard" mix of hip hop, reggae and African music with a political flavour that consciously eschews racist, sexist or materialistic music. As Kantako says, "Our music format is designed to resurrect the mind, not keep the mind asleep." He also plays "talking books" on black history, culture and liberation struggles that he receives from the audio service for the blind.

Another way that the micro-radio movement intrinsically challenges cultural hegemony is on the networking level. It is a model of organization concerned more with spreading information than with hierarchical control. In this regard, Kantako has even produced a 20 minute video on how to set up your own micro radio station, which he has distributed widely around the country to those wanting to get started. I recently asked Kantako what his vision was for the micro-radio movement, since it is a term he coined himself.

> I would like to see lots of little stations come on the air all over the country so you could drive out of one signal right into another. If you had a gap, you could run a tape until the next one came into range. I'm not interested in big megawatt stations. When you get too big, you get what you got now in America which is basically a homogenized mix of nothing, a bunch of mindless garbage which keeps the people operating in a mindless state. We think that the more community-based these things become, the more the community can put demands on the operators of these stations to serve the needs of that community.

So, I envision myself behind the wheel of my van, cruising the USA of the future with a map of micro-radio stations lighting my way from coast to coast, reflecting the wide array of cultural diversity that exists beneath the surface gloss — a vision that is the antithesis of the lockstep national unity of the new world order.

I smile broadly as I recall a recent radio interview with a community station in which Kantako was asked what he would do if the FCC came and took his equipment. "We're prepared," he said, "to be a mobile station until we get some equipment again. We can run our station off of a 10 speed bike if necessary." Then, when asked, "How can our listeners support you in your struggle? Should we write the FCC?," his reply was immediate. "Go on the air! Just go on the air!"

* * *

NOTES

1. The Federal Communications Commission is the official body charged with regulating the airwaves in the USA.
2. National Public Radio is a network of not-for-profit radio stations supported with a mix of corporate and government sponsorship.

11

The Feminist Radio Collective of Peru: Women...on the air

Tachi Arriola

I still laugh when I remember. We were in a meeting in Lima, at Las Manuelas, discussing what the radio station would be like — our radio station. We came from Iquitos, from Cajamarca, from the north and from the south, from the jungle, the mountains, the coast...from all over Peru. And there was something of everything: radio producers, journalists, feminist intellectuals, communications experts and, as a bonus, a publicist.

— The radio must represent all women's ways of thinking.
— But let's not forget a gender perspective...

Discussions and discussions. And just when one of us was summing up the day's conclusions, right at the best part of her speech, click, the cassette ran out. When it clicked, five of us jumped up to turn it over. When we got to the tape recorder that we were recording everything with, all five of us looked at each other. Nobody knew what to do, nobody knew how to work the blessed thing. How embarrassing! Great communicators, but we just stood there. After the confusion we all burst out laughing, the Miss Fix-its and the on-lookers. Moral of the day — you have to begin at the beginning.

It's important to think carefully about what a women's radio station would be like, but you need to come down to earth too. We didn't know anything about technical stuff and radio is, more than anything else, a technical thing. Philosophy is one thing. Nuts, bolts, plugs, mikes, the knobs on a tape recorder are something else. Some of us knew how to put a programme together, but handling the equipment was a "man's thing." We had left it up to them — that's how discrimination begins.

We were dreaming about, striving for, a radio of our own.

And we weren't the only ones with this dream. We were joined by Karen and a group of feminists from Denmark who were determined to make the project work. We wanted to set up not one, but three transmitters: in Lima, in Cusco, and in Trujillo. But Peru's a violent place, more and more so. And in that year of '89, after considering the situation, the funding organization thought it better to wait a bit. Maybe later.

A Peru-Chile regional project had been set up and they decided to begin with the Chile part. Radio Tierra in Santiago, run by the *compañeras* from La Morada is a result of that project. It was the first feminist radio station in Latin America. So, what about the Peruvians. We didn't have a radio station but we were together: five organizations with some radio experience and a mountain of enthusiasm. Why not keep at it? And that's how the Feminist Radio Collective was born.

Five organizations, each with its own style and flavour. The Flora Tristán Peruvian Women's Centre, named after a great social activist and feminist vanguard of the last century; the Manuela Ramos Movement, whose name isn't taken from any particular woman but represents all poor women; the Calandria Social Communicators Association, which had taken its name from that bird, the bearer of glad tidings, which plays such a symbolic role in Arguedas' writings.[1] These three organizations are from Lima, the capital, but Lima isn't all of Peru. The provinces played a role from the beginning. The *compañeras* from Trujillo, from the Micaela Bastidas Centre for Women's Advancement, were part of the collective. Micaela was Tupac Amaru's wife and just as revolutionary as he.[2] And from Cusco, the Amauta Centre for Women's Studies and Advancement, who produce their radio programmes in Quechua.

In fact, we are more than five organisations. Each of our groups is linked to other networks in the country, like the National Network of Rural Women with its twenty radio production teams who work with peasant women. It's strange that here, in spite of everything, more and more groups who work in or want to work in radio are springing up all the time. There is no end to the number of women who want to speak out, to give their opinions, to communicate with one another. I don't know if there are other countries like ours with so many problems and, at the same time, so much desire to speak out. The two are related, aren't they?

Well, we formed a collective. We were together, so now what? We came up with an ambitious plan of action: researching, producing, evaluating, training and everything that ends in 'ing', even vacillating! We wanted to do everything right now. We were raring to go. The truth is that everything was just on paper, all beautiful, all perfect. But, when we started to really get down to work, we found ourselves up against a brick wall. We realized we didn't know very much. We knew each other's names but we had hardly spoken to each other. We knew the names of the radio programmes that each group did, but we hadn't listened to them. Communicators...in-communicado.

So, the first thing was to get to know one another, listen to each other's programmes, criticize, evaluate, discover how we messed up, and what our errors were, and what successes we had in common. But we were afraid. More precisely, we were afraid of saying things as we saw them — directly and honestly. So, in order not to hurt anyone, we didn't say anything. But silence made people even more touchy. During that first year there was a lot of mistrust. There were moments of coolness, not to mention heated arguments. But our enthusiasm was greater than all this silliness and, bit by bit, we overcame it.

During this first stage we learned to trust each other, but we didn't produce any programmes as a group. We called ourselves a radio collective, but radio? No way. For the sake of doing something we produced a couple of pamphlets and held a national training workshop. In the workshop we discussed communications theories. We didn't do much concrete. Yes, we had a lot of meetings; up to two a month. And the collective's programmes? Very well, thanks.

Finally, in one of our many planning meetings someone said:

— "It's nearly November."
— "So?"
— "So November 25th is the Day of Non Violence Against Women."
— "Right on! We have to do something!"
— "Something equals nothing. What do you suggest?"
— "Listen girls... How about a radio campaign?"

And so, we started to 'do' radio. We started on the smallest scale, public service announcements. We call them "spots". But not traditional ones. We wanted to do something different, to draw attention. It was our first time in the arena and we wanted to shine. The topics would be the usual; rape, physical and sexual abuse. The challenge would be how we did it. Abstract, disapproving messages, all politically correct, would be no good. Let's be honest. Where do women experience violence? At home, at work, even in religious processions. So we came up with this spot:

> SOUND EFFECTS — *Women singing in a religious procession*
> MAN — *(pretending)* Pray for us sinners...
> WOMAN — Hey, mister,... what's the matter with you
> MAN — Ave Maria...Ave Mariiia..!
> WOMAN — I said don't push...You're a real smartass, aren't you? Well, we'll see!
> MAN — Oooooow! That hurts..!
> ANNOUNCER — The jerks are on the loose. Douse their flame where it causes pain!

They also feel us up on the buses. So, since the lambada was really popular at the time, we hit on the idea of using the same music to warn the nuisances. The slogan was "Remember, men. You don't dance the lambada on a minibus!"

Some were more lighthearted, some were more serious, but with our spots we were relating major feminist demands to everyday situations; rape, for example. We made one spot about assault and rape in the street and another about the kind that goes on at home. Then there's that taboo subject that scarcely gets talked about: rape committed by husbands when they come home drunk and force themselves on you. Even feminists wondered about those spots — they were a bit violent in their way of denouncing violence. So, what happened? Life is full of surprises, as Pedro Navaja sings. It turned out, when we distributed these announcements, that commercial stations accepted some and not others, according to their format. One station with a sensationalist bent, real redneck, took only two from us, the ones that dealt with rape. "Don't you have any more of these?", they said. "We want action, blood, impact!"

On November 25 those idiots broadcast the two famous spots, the heavy ones. Listener response was immediate. There was an uproar at the station. Women were in support. Men were calling in, mad at the station, accusing the announcers of being traitors, turncoats. There was a huge fuss. The announcers were happy because their ratings went up that day.

We were happy too. We wanted people to have opinions, to participate, to think about things.

These spots are like mosquitos. They sting, they go, they sting again. They're very effective on radio. So much so that when International Women's Day came around we repeated the whole thing.

> SOUND — *Scary music and street noises*
> MAN — Psst...Psst...hey, baby.
> WOMAN — What's the matter with you?
> MAN — What a body, what legs, what curves...!
> WOMAN — Leave me alone, don't bug me.
> MAN — What eyes, what a mouth, what a cutie..!
> WOMAN — Cutie? Karate!
> *(Karate blows from her, howls from him)*
> ANNOUNCER — For every turkey, there's a Christmas.

The situation in Peru is really difficult. And that's exactly why you have to spice life up a bit, inspire some hope. That March we had been traumatized by the brutal assassinations of popular leaders. Maria Elena Moyano, president of the Villa El Salvador Women's Federation had been one of them. The *Senderistas*[3] killed her and blew up her body with dynamite. There were threats, danger was in the air. Faced with this, our programmes, our spots, adopted a different tone. The conditions under which we lived forced us to maintain a difficult balance between humorous messages which give courage to listeners and those which denounce the tragic situation facing our people.

Now the collective is producing radio shows. And by producing —and evaluating — we've realized that we need to learn more. We're conscious of the need to get more training so we can be more professional. We're clear about the feminist line, the theory. But we don't know how to communicate it very well. We need a method, a more appropriate format. There's no other way.

We have to learn about everything. As I said, as far as technical stuff goes, we were nowhere. We didn't know if a turntable was for eating off, or for playing records. So, since the Chilean women were training their technicians in order to get Radio Tierra on the air, several of our compañeras packed their bags and were off to Santiago. Jimena was one of them and now she's an expert in mixing. She can put in sound effects, lay down music beds, add in whatever she thinks of. There she is, sitting in front of the control board, the Belle of Trujillo.

Now we're organizing the third national workshop for women radio producers. The methodology is simple: learn by doing, learn from your errors, or from your "horrors", as Rosita said. You learn to do interviews, sociodramas, reports, soap operas — not as rigid models, cold, removed from life, but mixing feminist principles with the rules of communication: "what?" and "how?"

And speaking of communication, we began to be more and more concerned with the public, with the audience. What's happening with our listeners? Are we reaching them? What do we know about them, about their lives, their tastes, their language? Communication has to be two way and perhaps we, in our haste, were going down a one way street. So we've begun to do studies, to research, to learn more about what's going on with women — women in the country, in the city, migrant women. How are we understood by a woman from the sandpits,[4] living in a straw shack with a child on her back and a pitcher of water on her head. We want to reach them. We want to learn about them. We need to make our programme about them.

This means participation. It's absolutely necessary that the collective becomes a place where women can have their say, where, through the programmes of the various networks, women can hear each other, complain, suggest, tell their troubles and share their joys. I want to emphasize the latter, joy, because there is already enough sadness. And peace, because Peru lives — or survives — amidst violence. There are bullets, but there is also hunger, unemployment, cholera, and repression coming from above and from below.

So here we are, without much experience, but with a lot of desire. Two years' work is really not a lot, and yet it is a lot. It's not an easy thing to create unity, to coordinate, to do things collectively. We want to grow. Now there are five of us. Five is a beginning. We have to continue to make links with other groups of women from all over the country who are involved in radio. We need to make connections outside Peru, with Latin American *compañeras,* or even with women from other continents who are in the same struggle.

We haven't lost the dream that brought us together — our own radio station — because in this society women are always in second place. I remember once a respected communicator asked us, "Why a women's radio station?...Communication is by all and for all. Or do you want to go it alone?"

No, it's not a question of going it alone, of separating men and women, not even as a joke! Men work in several of our programmes, as producers, as announcers. We don't want to implement reverse discrimination. But women's experience continues to be silenced and manipulated by the media. If the general public is not aware of this, if women's specific demands do not become the concern of all people, if they are not as popular as the last soap opera or as much discussed as the next soccer game, we're not going anywhere. That's why we formed the feminist radio collective, to engage many women — and many men — in the struggle for women's rights. And that's why the perspective of our programme is a woman's perspective, and so is the control. What are we still, on the TV screen or behind the mike? Decorative objects or advertising come-ons. You can count on one hand the women who run a magazine, a television channel, a radio station.

That's the heart of the matter — power. Who has it? Those who have initiative, ideas, those who make decisions. But also, and most importantly, those who own the media. It's this ownership that must be democratized. That's why we want a women's radio station. To overturn macho history...now that we know how to turn over a cassette!

* * *

NOTES

1. Arguedas is a Peruvian writer. While he writes in Spanish, his best-known work makes use of the rhythms of the indigenous Quechua language.
2. Tupac Amaru was an Incan leader murdered by the Spanish.
3. Senderistas — Members of *Sendero Luminoso* (Shining Path), a Peruvian guerrilla army
4. Lima is surrounded on three sides by a desert. The sandpits surrounding the city are populated with millions of Peruvian peasants, displaced from their land and looking for work in the city.

PART III: DEVELOPMENT

Contemporary understanding of development sees it as a complex process through which people can increasingly gain control over their material and social environments in order to meet their own needs. In this view, people must be able to take part in making decisions that will affect their futures, and real development cannot take place without the participation of all social sectors.

The four chapters in this section look at examples of how community radio has been able to contribute to a participatory process of development. In their examinations, the authors have attempted to identify some of the factors contributing to the success or failure of the projects.

12

The Hard Lesson of Autonomy: Kayes Rural Radio

Pascal Berqué

A leaflet circulates among the community of immigrants from Mali now living in France:

> You have heard of the rural radio station in Kayes. For the past three years, this radio has given a voice to the village populations. It was a training and information tool for the entire Kayes region. Those of us who have left the Kayes region want the radio to continue to live. We have created a support group to allow this to happen.

"These words move us," said the Italian coordinators of the project. "Could we have asked for anything more when we designed the Kayes rural radio many years ago?"

In 1982 Italian cooperation agencies set up the *Sahel Program*, to work with countries of the Sahel region of Africa in their struggle against desertification of the land. They asked the governments of Senegal, Mali, Burkina Faso, and Niger to identify one zone within each country in which it would be possible to initiate an integrated rural development programme. In Mali, the choice was the Kayes region. An animation and training programme for rural development was launched there in 1987. Two Italian non-governmental organizations, Terranuova and Gao, were the promoters and managers of the programme, and the Kayes rural radio was the central component.

AN ALTERNATIVE TO TRADITIONAL AGRICULTURAL INSTRUCTION

The decision to opt for a radio station, rather than a traditional training programme, was influenced not only by political considerations, but also by the geographic, social and economic reality of the region.

First, the geography:

Being geographically isolated remains the region's major problem. Within a vast area, four hundred villages are linked by footpaths in the dry season. In the rainy season they are isolated from each other. A traditional training programme would have had to limit its scope to the few accessible villages along the river bank.

Next, the social situation:

The Soninkés, who have traditionally been involved in trade activities, are the dominant ethnic group in the region. Since the 1960s large numbers of Soninkés have emigrated to France. This social dynamic had contributed to a cultural openness which would support the work of a rural radio station.

Finally, the economic situation:

The region's economy is a subsistence one, based primarily on agriculture and livestock. In this context, the large emigrant community plays an important role in supporting the families living in the rural zones by sending money regularly. This process, which began in the early 1960s, is a major social phenomenon in the region. The emigrants, who have organized villagers' groups and associations abroad, have promoted a series of significant interventions in the social sector (health, village water projects), and in the productive sector (irrigation projects); these activities are in stark contrast to the absence of any government initiatives in the region.

Terranuova and Gao first attempted to better familiarize themselves with the social fabric of the Kayes region. A survey of four hundred villages allowed them to reach over 3,500 people, including village leaders, young people and women. They discovered no fewer that 308 organizations of all kinds, more or less structured, of which 185 were emigrant associations. While a number of these groups appear and disappear quickly, most of the villages have an emigrants' association abroad, which supports local initiatives for social development: schools, dispensaries, mosques. Some of these associations work together to support larger initiatives, all the while tackling the problem of developing projects that are more production-oriented.

Certain improvements in traditional practices, supported by a moderate use of the emigrants' contributions, can help increase production, but only as long as local production costs are lower than those of the market. A rural radio station can not only support these actions, but present them in a way that will stimulate other, similar actions. One of the ideas behind the project was that the funds provided by the emigrants of the Kayes region could be invested in social and production-oriented projects and that the value of these projects could be evaluated not by technicians, but by the people themselves. The Kayes radio station was to be a channel that would allow this evaluation.

The original idea to establish a radio station was reinforced by the findings of the village surveys and the better understanding of the nature of the region. The general popularity of radio in Africa was another factor in the decision to establish a radio project. There were already radio receivers in the villages and radio was the only modern means of communication integrated into the daily routines of the villagers. There remained one essential problem: the scarcity, if not total absence, of programming in local languages.

Both local and rural, the Kayes station was intended from the beginning to contribute to the social and productive development of the prefectures of Kayes and Yeliman. The station is located in the region and broadcasts in local languages, unlike the national service of Radio-télévision malienne (RTM) — which broadcasts exclusively from Bamako, the capital, and primarily in French.

HOW TO WORK WITH EXISTING AUTHORITIES

The task of identifying, informing and preparing the various players in a rural radio project is a long one requiring very special care and respect for local customs and existing power structures.

In Africa, rural radio is supposed to stay strictly within the bounds of supporting local social and economic development. It is not supposed to be concerned with political and ideological matters. However, the unstated political purpose of the Kayes station included support for peasant organizations and, at the same time, a transformation of the authoritarian nature of relations between the local communities and central authorities. To be a truly democratic tool, the radio would support peasant associations, acting both as their spokesperson and a point of reference.

Studies undertaken in preparation for the project identified a number of organizations in the Kayes region. L'Union Régionale des Coopératives Agricoles de Kayes (URCAK — Regional Union of Agricultural Cooperatives in Kayes) was a strong peasant organization in the irrigated area alongside the river. Equally dynamic grassroots organizations were also identified in the interior zones. Contrasting with these small and active organizations, was the training organization Opération Vallée du Sénégal, de la Térékolé et du lac Magui (OVSTM), an organization with a hundred workers deprived of both initiative and ability for action.

One solution would have been for the peasants' activities to benefit from the technical capacity of OVSTM without funding this costly training machine. But the government of Mali did not want to hear anything of the sort. It clearly demanded that the Italian organizations provide priority funding for OVSTM.

In the end, the participating organizations were able to refuse this demand, on the one hand thanks to terms of the contract agreed to by the government and, on the other hand, to the prestige of the peasant organizations, especially that of URCAK, with whom the final agreements were signed directly.

The Italian NGOs' choice to work directly with the peasant organizations represents the strength, but in a way, also the weakness of the integrated rural development programme in the Kayes region: Strength because of the coherence of the overall organization which supports production and social activities and accentuates a grassroots infrastructure, and weakness because once the contract was signed with URCAK, the government of Mali did not show much interest in the project.

Kayes Rural Radio was a novelty in a radio landscape subject to monopoly rule, with only one national station and no regional stations at all. Convincing those in charge of Mali's radio and television broadcasting corporation (RTM) to support the project was the first difficult task. Their agreement was essential since they had the authority to decide whether the Kayes project would receive permission to broadcast, and the project depended on their technical expertise.

In the end, RTM granted permission and provided three technicians and a promise that the person in charge of the rural animation section would visit the project periodically. Further collaboration is foreseen in programme exchanges and in an overall evaluation of the Kayes project.

RTM was much more interested by the experience of Kayes to the extent that it could serve to support RTM's plan to overhaul rural radio on a national scale. RTM's programming is still anchored in the traditional model of instruction, a model conceived essentially as a means of transmitting the directives of the central authorities for modernizing agriculture and livestock farming.

PROGRAMMES, MANAGEMENT AND DEVELOPMENT

On August 1, 1988, the Kayes radio station officially went on the air. Broadcasting starts each day at 9:00 a.m. and continues to 3:00 p.m. It returns to the air at 8:00 p.m. and the broadcast day ends at 10:30.

The skills, training and experience of programme producers at the Kayes radio station are very different from those of traditional communication specialists. Kayes' producers are people from the region with minimal technical qualifications and no radio experience. They are recommended for participation in the project by the social groups, grassroots associations or villagers' assemblies. They follow a theoretical and practical training programme in the use of different methods of radio communication.

Ever since the project was conceived, it has been held that rural radio must rely on the experiences learned from development and not on traditional mass communication techniques.

In its first phase the radio concentrated on those already involved in various social and production-oriented development activities: village spokespeople, social groups, grassroots cooperatives. The next phase sought to incorporate social actors whose essential role in development was recognized, but who are not well-represented on an organizational level — women for example. The station was also intended to support the process of transforming social structures, strengthening their more dynamic elements, and contributing to the elimination of obstacles arising from rigid traditional hierarchies.

But it is difficult to change attitudes. People had not received anything but administrative messages from the authorities. In this context, the station's use of local languages was a key factor for mutual understanding.

The programmes were produced in Soninké, the language spoken by 85% of the local rural population; in Bambara, the majority language on a national scale; in Kassonké, a language spoken in certain parts of the Kayes region; and in Peuhl, the language of the shepherds.

At Kayes, direct audience participation is encouraged by dealing with issues of primary concern to the daily lives of the listeners. Training aims to avoid didactic presentations and abstract technical references. The resultant programmes take the real interests of the listeners into account. The programming includes the following:

- *Historical and cultural programmes* strengthen cultural identity. They are based upon the differences between people's experiences, oral history and documentary information. The cultural and artistic heritage of the various social groups is highlighted by recording songs, dances, and traditional events in the different villages. Theatrical and artistic groups in the region also produce radio pieces.

- *Educational programmes* increase the degree of individual and social autonomy, and support collective management abilities. Literacy courses in Soninké and Bambara, accompanied by a parallel literacy campaign in the villages, are the best example of this type of programming.

- *News programmes* support social and economic transformation processes with clear, simple and precise news on a variety of subjects: weather, market information, transportation and health.

- *Development-type programmes* disseminate information about innovative experiences which can be easily reproduced. These programmes cover projects which have been carried out in the region (mills, granaries, solar dryers, village pharmacies), and outside projects of importance, such as agro-forestry (reforestation, the introduction of new types of production, the protection of forest cultures); cottage industry production (support for traditional agricultural activities, experimenting with new techniques).

The radio station becomes a source of news and examples. The testimonies broadcast over the air are credible and inspire change precisely because of the radio's physical proximity. People seek out the source of information and try to understand the proposed approaches. This is not the least of the advantages of this new communication tool. But this "local" radio also attracts a great deal of interest thousands of kilometres away, among emigrants from Mali in France. Their enthusiasm grows during vacations in the villages, where they benefit from news in their national language, and a connection with the activities of their associations. The exchange and broadcast of cassettes fosters a new type of contact.

A DESIRE TO READ

Rural radio must create a desire to read. This assertion, which may seem paradoxical at first, is integral to the literacy programmes, one of the Kayes radio station's essential activities. After two years of broadcasting literacy radio programmes in local languages, the station began producing simple texts in local languages to offer to the newly-literate listeners of the radio. This extension of the radio programmes is fundamental, as even the best methods amount to nothing without follow-up. On this subject, Adrian Adams writes:

> Literacy is not a natural demand, it does not come from the self. In a context where it (literacy) does not simplify approaches to administrators, leads to no diploma, provides no right to employment, and does not yield access to the press or to literature, it can have the appearance of a path for second-class citizens, indeed, as another interference in village life. Teaching people to read is but the first step, the least difficult step. What is more difficult is to make reading worthwhile. To enhance literacy in Soninké is, by definition, to produce writing in Soninké which responds to the needs and desires of the newly literate. So many literacy programmes around the world have failed at this stage. Rural radio must create a desire to read, to learn, a belief in the usefulness of the written word.

In fact, rural radio must foster a climate which gives value to literacy in local languages. Disseminating works for the newly-literate contributes to this.

CRISIS MANAGEMENT

The Kayes rural radio is presently confronted by a both financial and statutory crisis.

From 1987 to 1989, it benefitted from the financial and technical support provided by Italian NGOs and expatriate Italian personnel. Seventy percent of the project budget was used to set up the station's infrastructure.

In 1989, Italian NGO activities from a general blockage. Mali's request for an extension of the rural radio project thus remains up in the air. The NGO, Gao, invested its own resources for a few months before resolving to look for transitory solutions. What to do? Close the station while waiting for funds from Italy? Or continue programming while at the same time mobilizing local and national resources? This latter solution was chosen.

Four associations created a management committee and set about gathering local and national resources. RTM offered to keep its three technicians; telephone costs were to be paid by the Ministry of Communication; employees' salaries were reduced; Gao tried its best to find other sources of material support; electrical costs were frozen by the local authorities and each of the four organizations on the management committee agreed to furnish a monthly fee. In the short term, closing the station was avoided, but the prolongation of the crisis meant that not all of the commitments were respected. At the end of May 1991, the telephone was cut off and the energy supply was threatened by non-payment of bills. Only the associations on the management committee and Gao honoured their obligations. The Italian NGO was confident that the funds from Italy, promised in March 1991, would guarantee funding for three years. But as of February 1992, the money was still unavailable.

The crisis showed that the radio station would not give up out of indifference. The peasants have organized and the emigrant associations are organizing in France. But a viable long-term solution remains to be found. Part of this solution will have to be institutional. The Kayes radio station suffers from the absence of a clear legal framework specifying management structures, the role of the grassroots associations, the role of the State... The associations involved in this radio adventure are unwilling to pursue their commitments without statutory guarantees. No specific legislation for this type of radio exists.

At any rate, the situation is evolving in light of major policy changes underway in Mali. "Free radio" is in the process of being authorized. A decree governing the medium is one of the consequences of a national conference on information and communication, held December 19-24, 1991, in Bamako.

The usefulness of Kayes radio for local development is recognized by all the partners involved. Both the local participants and their Italian partners are aware of the stakes and constraints of autonomy. Autonomy can cost a lot in terms of reduced funding, materials, human resources and technical support. Independence comes at this price.

THE LONG-TERM BET

The troubles of Kayes Rural Radio are classic. They are those of an independent radio station confronted by the need to find funding. But they also involve two other constraints: first, an extremely precarious regional and national economic situation; and secondly, the difficulty of being an international development project. It is a paradoxical situation. But after the first years of material and financial aid, the continuation of any cooperative project becomes complex. In the present case, the help of the last Italian funds will allow the station to benefit from a delayed deadline, in order to prepare itself for full autonomy — a task which must be undertaken immediately.

The Kayes rural radio is betting on the long-term. Approaches to potential partners, coupled with research into all possible funding sources, is essential. There are the fees from rural collectives and emigrant associations, RTM, Ministries and their technical services, Gao and other Italian support, as well as from international bodies such as UNESCO and UNSO, with whom radio production agreements have been signed. Finally, there is the broadcasting of paid announcement and communiqués. There are plans to establish a print shop, necessary for the production of booklets in national languages. And one more original idea has come to light: emigrants in France can now pay for messages and communiqués sent by fax to the station. These messages are then relayed over the airwaves of Kayes radio. Distances are thus shortened and time is saved.

These actions ensure a minimal operational budget, but are not enough to guarantee real autonomy. Luckily, Italian support will continue, but this time more than ever, there must be an awareness of its inevitable withdrawal in 1993. Radio is a powerful communication tool, and its potential must be made known to the numerous international cooperation projects being conducted locally. A systematic approach in this direction is being developed.

In January 1992, an association was formed, l'Association des radiodiffuseurs de Kayes (ARKDR — Kayes Broadcasting Association). It brings together all the other organizations associated with the project along with the technical services of the various organisations charged with rural development in the area. This association, united in crisis, crystallized the will of all the partners fighting to conserve this development tool and to continue the actions undertaken — taking into account the economic realities of the station.

Kayes Rural Radio has passed the experimental stage and become a real training and information tool in the hands of the village organizations. This rare case in Africa is a precious example, rich in experience, which we will have to know how to take advantage of.

* * *

DOCUMENTARY SOURCE MATERIAL

Giordano Sivini (1991), *Les origines de la radio rurale de Kayes en tant qu'instrument de dévelopment*, Gao Coopération Internationale; Université de Calabre.

Ada Cavazzani (1989), *Une radio rurale à Kayes*, Gao Coopération Internationale; Université de Calabre.

Radio rurale de Kayes (1990), *Lettres d'auditeurs de la radio rurale de Kayes* (1988-1990); ORDIK.

Ladji Niangane, Journées nationales de réflexions sur l'information et la communication du 19 au 24 décembre 1991.

Adrien Adams, Remarques sur les débuts de l'alphabétisation en langue soninké par la radio rurale de Kayes.

13

Mahaweli Community Radio

MJR David

The first of its kind in South Asia, Sri Lanka's Mahaweli Community Radio (MCR) was set up in 1981 by the Sri Lanka Broadcasting Corporation (SLBC) with the assistance of the United Nations Educational Scientific and Cultural Organization (UNESCO) and the Danish International Development Agency (DANIDA). Now considered a prototype for the region, the project was largely initiated and implemented through international cooperation. The MCR experience provides a base to discuss the positive as well as the negative influences of international cooperation in setting up community radio, particularly in the South Asian Region.

This article looks first at the origin, philosophy, approach and mode of operation of MCR with reference to the role played by the foreign collaborators. Following that, the current situation will be reviewed before considering some of the positive and negative aspects of foreign funding in a project of this nature. Lessons that could be learned in relation to foreign collaboration and funding in setting up community radio projects, particularly in the South Asian region, will be discussed at the conclusion.

THE ORIGINS OF MCR

A new government had recently come to power in Sri Lanka and in 1979 its number one priority was a programme to divert the Mahaweli River — a huge irrigation scheme involving the resettlement of approximately one million people from all over the country. In the same year Knud Ebbesen, a Danish broadcaster with experience in the public access department of the Danish Broadcasting Corporation, was on a private visit to Sri Lanka. Ebbesen sensed that this was an opportune moment to propose a participatory radio project for Sri Lanka. The Mahaweli Community Radio Project would be set up alongside the river diversion project, to facilitate the socio-economic development of the settlers.

Fortunately at the time of making this proposal Dr. Sarath Amunugama, a reputed communication scholar who advocated two-way participatory communication, was Permanent Secretary to the Ministry of State which looked into matters pertaining to mass media. The Director General of SLBC, the late Thevis Guruge and the Deputy Director General, the late E.S.T. Fernando, who was later appointed as overall coordinator of MCR, were also most willing to support the project. According to Choy Arnaldo (1990) of UNESCO, the support of these people was a major contributing factor to the initiation of MCR.

UNESCO and DANIDA provided the initial capital for the project and ongoing costs were to be provided by SLBC. Total foreign funding received for the project was US$1.1 million (UNESCO, 1990).

A FORUM FOR PEOPLE

The MCR concept was a modified version of the experience of *Baandvaerkstedet* — the Tape Workshop, a public access programme of Radio Denmark. *Baandvaerkstedet* teams provided technical and production support to individuals and community groups so that they could produce their own radio programmes for broadcast on Radio Denmark's national service.

While the MCR project made a large number of significant adaptations to the Danish experience, MCR proponents were convinced that radio's contribution to the socio-economic development of the settlers would only be realized if they facilitated the listeners' participation in the programming.

This participation warranted a radical departure from SLBC's conventional practices. The new production techniques required investments in transportation and new recording equipment modified for use in the countryside. They also required expertise in field production techniques that were unknown in Sri Lanka. In this way, international cooperation was a pre-requisite to setting up MCR.

The MCR philosophy has developed within the last decade. The following are the major guidelines that could be identified at the time of writing.

1. The urban elitist orientation of radio should be minimized if not eradicated. Mahaweli Community Radio could contribute towards this by providing opportunities for rural listeners to voice their opinions.
2. Because rural life should be approached as a whole, any subject relevant to rural life can become a programme theme.
3. Maximum possible access to all sections and points of view on development issues should be given to create an atmosphere for constructive discussion and inter-community communications.
4. Programmes should be conceptualized not on the basis of what the producers think, but on field research findings.
5. Listeners are pleased to have their own kith and kin visiting their homes through the "speaking box" (radio) rather than strangers. Thus, innovations are more likely to be adapted when someone with similar socio-economic standing conveys them. This is best provided for in an exchange of experiences rather than a lecture or monologue.
6. The ability to participate in this exchange of views helps listeners see their own potential and responsibility in the realization of development goals.
7. Maximum effect of local community radio is achieved when target groups are well-defined.
8. Development is not something that radio can achieve alone. Radio should be part of an overall strategy. Therefore, Mahaweli Community Radio works in close harmony and coordination with other media and other organizations.

MODE OF OPERATIONS: POTS, PANS AND THE MICROPHONE TO THE VILLAGE

Two methods are used to operationalize the above mentioned guidelines. The first method, used since the inception of the project in 1981, involves mobile teams travelling to the villages. Later, in 1985, the first local community radio station was established in Girandurukotte, one of the Mahaweli Settlement villages. A second local community station was set up on an experimental basis at Kotmale in the upper Mahaweli area in 1989. The field-visit production teams, comprised of two producers and a cook, go to a village and spend four days there, often staying at a public place such as the village temple or community development centre. They explore the socio-economic and even psychological realities of village life. Once the producers gather first-hand knowledge on a given theme, they make their recordings. They then return to their studio to prepare for the third week.

In the third week a larger production team of producers, technical officers and assistants returns to the village. They carry with them a mobile console and other recording equipment. During the previous week the villagers have been organizing a cultural show for recording by the production team. Local participation in these shows is very high; sometimes more than 120 people present music, theatre and poetry in a show lasting six to eight hours.

Following the cultural show, the producers stay in the village to edit the programme, inviting local people to help shape the final programme — a mix of the cultural show and the interviews from the first week. The final programme is later broadcast on the regional service of SLBC.

One criticism about the MCR method of operation is that it is too costly and thus not suitable for a developing country such as Sri Lanka. As one high ranking SLBC officer commented, the Muslim Service is able to produce a one hour weekly programme using existing resources, but the MCR field teams require a large amount of additional resources and financing to produce a programme of the same duration. While the difference can be accounted for by the fact that the Muslim service production is studio-based and MCR field-based, critics are quick to point out that MCR's mode of operations can only last as long as foreign funding is available.

There can be little dispute that the MCR operations at the initial stages were costly, and that the very nature of participatory community broadcasting demands more resources than studio production. However, through a process of experimentation, cost has been brought down to a level where MCR may be able to operate without foreign funding. At the initial stage when three weekly half hour programmes were broadcast (1981-1985), a programme hour cost about US $250 — about ten times more than the usual cost of a programme hour of the regional stations. However by using new formats, mixing village productions with studio productions and attaching production teams to regional stations, the cost was brought down to about US $37.50 per hour. At the Girandurukotte station a programme hour was produced at a recurrent cost of about US $35.00.

One may ask why low cost production techniques could not have been implemented from the very beginning. For instance why were local community radios, which are less costly then field visits, not introduced at the beginning? There appear to be two primary reasons for this. First, if local community radios were proposed at the very beginning, a monopolistic institution like the SLBC would probably have rejected the idea of community radio wholesale. By introducing the concept on a gradual basis MCR was able to survive within the framework of SLBC. Secondly, the early years of MCR were experimental and experimental projects are more costly than conventional ones.

CRISIS: THE PROJECT AT THE CROSSROADS

Within the period 1981-1989, MCR's mobile teams visited some 1,500 villages. Surveys and studies have revealed the extent of MCR's impact in the region. Girandurukotte Community Radio and the MCR broadcasts on the Anuradhapura regional service are listened to by about 90 percent of the local population and are the second most important source of agricultural and health-related information. Within a decade of its inception, the MCR project had expanded to reach almost the entire Sinhala-speaking rural population. Community radio teams with mobile recording and editing facilities were stationed at all regional stations. A cadre of local broadcasters who were adequately qualified, trained and committed to the project had developed.

However, not everything was going well with the project and problems became apparent when the international funding and assistance ran out in 1990. The project had failed to gain long- lasting support from SLBC and there was a high degree of disorganization. Political violence was one reason for this disorganization. In 1988, at the height of violence in southern Sri Lanka, about 100 extra-judicial killings per day were taking place. Obviously community radio gets disorganized in such an atmosphere. However, the root cause of the disorganization of the MCR was not political violence.

The Second UNESCO Regional Seminar was an attempt to discuss the future of the project. Evelyne Foy, (1991) General Secretary of AMARC, participated in the seminar and observed a situation that was far from encouraging:

> An evaluation of the current state of MCR by the local producers raised a number of problems: the difficulty of

keeping resources intended for MCR within the project, a general lack of local resources, and centralization of decision-making in the capital and in the head offices of the Sri Lanka Broadcasting System.

However, a degree of optimism has surfaced as Knud Ebbesen recently visited Sri Lanka to assist the Ministry for Information in filing a proposal to establish an autonomous institutional structure for community radio in Sri Lanka. The proposal is being studied and there are strong indications that it will receive government approval. However, at the time of this writing the morale of MCR broadcasters is low, community radio units attached to the regional stations are in a state of disintegration, air time has been reduced and field visits have been greatly cut back. The two local community radios are functioning but with reduced momentum.

THE PROS AND CONS OF FOREIGN FUNDING AND INTERNATIONAL COOPERATION

It is important to investigate how things changed so dramatically once foreign funding started to withdraw. A more complete understanding of this problem might be gained by further considering the plus and minus points of foreign funding and international cooperation.

As mentioned earlier the MCR project was largely a foreign initiative made possible by the availability of international funding and because foreign collaborators were able to convince personalities engaged in policy-making and managing radio. It appears that in the establishment of community radio in South Asia, where broadcast media are State-controlled and highly centralized, some intervention of respected international agencies such as UNESCO and DANIDA can play a positive role.

Although a few personalities in the top management of SLBC supported community radio from the very beginning, there was opposition from many who were engaged in conventional broadcasting. The US $1.1 million received from the donor agencies not only provided financial strength, but also provided a degree of autonomy that shielded the MCR project management from those who opposed community radio. The MCR project enjoyed a degree of autonomy far exceeding that of any other programme service of SLBC. This autonomy provided an atmosphere for the programme producers to work freely.

International cooperation helped MCR to exist with minimum political interference. In a country where broadcasting is highly politicized, keeping out of politics is an important achievement. Without it credibility wears out and the survival of the project under successive governments becomes difficult. The partnership of UNESCO and DANIDA, which required political neutrality, could be cited among the various factors contributing to MCR's "apolitical" performance.

Another plus of international cooperation was that the MCR concept received wide recognition in the international setting and was adapted for other national settings. According to Ebbesen, the MCR experience has been widely used for an integrated rural development project in Bangladesh. Wijayananda Jayaweera, a pioneer of MCR and later a UNESCO consultant has used the MCR experience in developing and setting up rural broadcast systems in Bhutan and Cambodia.

In a sense the entire MCR exercise is an experiment in community radio, a new medium in South Asia. With the MCR experience the region gained a community radio model that has been tested and proven workable and which, with appropriate modifications, can and has been used in other national settings. It is largely because of the international agencies that the MCR project has become a model for the region and not only Sri Lanka.

What are the negative implications of international cooperation? The most prominent negative influence on MCR was an over-dependence on foreign support. After ten years the MCR project had come to operate as if the funding would always be there, and had not developed an appropriate plan in preparation for the withdrawal of international support.

That MCR has not developed into a self-supporting and commercially viable entity is another negative aspect of over-dependence on foreign funding. Presently the only source of earnings is the income gained from commercials at Girandurukotte Community Radio. Ten years of dependence on foreign funding has not helped MCR diversify its sources of funding and explore alternatives.

A more subtle, but nevertheless important factor, is the attitude that international funding encouraged within SLBC. While on the one hand foreign support brought a degree of autonomy to the project, it also led to SLBC's belief that the project was the responsibility of UNESCO and DANIDA. At the end of the final phase of the project there were only some sketchy proposals to create an autonomous, institutional structure for community radio. Nothing solid had materialized and MCR was in a very vulnerable position.

CONCLUDING CONSIDERATIONS

The crisis which MCR is facing may simply be the period of disorganization which most projects face at the time of transition. However, it still provides two important insights into the role of international cooperation in setting up sustainable community radio, particularly in the South Asian region.

The first insight is that MCR's failure to win long-lasting support within SLBC may be related to factors inherent in Asian broadcasting traditions. According to Felix Librero, "Asian broadcasting systems were originally organized as means of propagating government thinking and were designed to simply inform the people."

A project such as MCR which attempts to open a two-way communication process in the midst of such a system will inevitably run into opposition. There is no alternative to facing this reality. One way of facing it is to have a system where listeners are actively involved in the management of community radio. Whenever the guardians of the conventional broadcast system stand in the way of community radio, the listeners would speak up and support their station. Listener clubs are one promising way of involving the communities in this way.

The second lesson to be learned from the MCR experience is that coming up with plans on how to permanently institutionalize a community radio project, must be considered as the collective responsibility of the international agencies as well as the receiving organization. Designing a plan for the withdrawal of funding agencies is at least as important as initiating a project. Such a plan needs expertise and should be implemented well before funding is withdrawn. The international agencies should provide the expertise while the receiving organization should take the initiative of drawing up such a plan.

As the MCR experience demonstrates, in establishing community radios in Sri Lanka and most probably in South Asia, international cooperation is something that should be welcomed. However, maximum utilization of international cooperation can be made only if the international agencies and the national organizations define their roles and act accordingly.

* * *

DOCUMENTARY SOURCE MATERIAL

Aabenhuse, Ole (1985) "One-way and two-way systems in broadcasting." *Community Radio and Rural Development: Four Essays*, Mahaweli Community Radio.

Arnaldo, Carlos (1990) Opening remarks. *Second UNESCO Regional Seminar on Community Broadcasting in South East Asia and the Mahaweli Community Radio Project*, Kandy, Sri Lanka.

David, M.J.R. and Felix Librero (1991) *Radio's role in Rural Development; A case analysis of Mahaweli Community Radio, Sri Lanka.* Thesis submitted to the University of Philippines at Los Banos, Laguna, Philippines.

David, M.J.R. (1986) *An evaluative study of the impact of a settlement-based community radio.* Girandurokotte Community Radio.

Fernando, E.S.T. (1990) "Origin and Development of Mahaweli Community Radio." Paper presented at the *Regional Workshop on Community Broadcasting and New Technologies.* Malaysia.

Foy, E. (1991) "A difficult birth for C.R. in Sri Lanka." *InteRadio*, 2 (3).

Gunaratna, Rohan (1990) *Sri Lanka: A Lost Revolution.* Institute of Fundamental Studies, Kandy, Sri Lanka.

Hewage, Wijedasa (1990) "Mahaweli Community Radio." Paper presented at the *Regional seminar and Workshop in South East Asia and the Mahaweli Community Radio Project.* Sri Lanka.

Jayaweera, Wijayananda (1986) *Experiences in two-way communication.* Mahaweli Community Radio, Colombo, Sri Lanka.

Karunanayake, N. (1990) *Sixty-six years of broadcasting in Sri Lanka.* Center for Media and Policy Studies, Sri Lanka.

Librero, Felix (1991) "Hidden Problems of Community Radio in Asia." *InteRadio* 3 (2).

Mahaweli Community Radio (1985) *The MCR Work Book.* Edited by Ole Aabenhuse and Wijayananda Jayaweera. Mahaweli Community Radio, Sri Lanka.

14

Pluralist responses for Africa

Eugénie Aw

An experimental project in participatory radio communication was set up recently in a rural area of Africa. The development project, which used collective radio listening and encouraged active feedback, had succeeded in making the residents of the area aware of the importance of having a voice and of listening to each other, of hearing their neighbours on the radio, and of controlling communication. Perhaps, some might think, it was too successful.

By the time the technicians came from the capital to dismantle and take away the transmitter, the peasants had decided they liked controlling their own communication. Defiant of the authorities who wanted to take this newfound power from them, they had hidden *their* radio station.

Africa is watching the birth of a new movement for change. Some call it democratization, others, exasperation. People across the continent are reclaiming the right to participate, the right to a decent life, and the right to freedom of expression.

The written media have made a lot of progress and there is now a proliferation of private and opposition periodicals available. Radio, as the most widespread medium in Africa, will have a central role to play in this popular participation. However, totalitarian regimes and monolithic one-party systems are reluctant to loosen their grasp on the medium which for them remains a privileged means of disseminating propaganda. But their grip is beginning to slacken and the voices demanding more open policies for radio are getting stronger. In Mali, for example, a March, 1991 demonstration against the dictatorship was met with a show of force by the military. Following the conflict, the State radio refused to allow their airwaves to be used to call paramedics to the scene to treat the injured. Just under a year later, a free radio station was broadcasting legally in the capital city of Bamako.

According to Samba Touré, director of the Inter-African Center for Studies in Rural Radio at Ouagadougou, Burkina Faso (CIERRO):

> The need that's felt for the written press is even stronger when it comes to radio broadcasting, because radio affects the majority of the population. In the coming years radio broadcasting will follow in the footsteps of this unstoppable movement for change in our countries, and will be freed from the shackles of the State. Radio has the ability to address people in the languages they speak every day...This is a very important factor. (AMARC, 1991)

Rural radio addresses the majority of the population and tends to be more in tune with local realities. The World Association of Community Radio Broadcasters (AMARC) first took an active interest in African rural radio in 1989 when it made contact with CIERRO, in order to conduct a survey defining the parameters of participatory radio in Africa.

This study on rural and local radio in Africa was undertaken at a time when powerful movements for democratization and pluralism were being born. It aimed to fulfil what was at the time just a dream — to learn more about radio in the hands of citizens, radio in the service of local people and communities.

The work was completed in 1990 with a set of recommendations that included proposals to increase popular participation. These and other recommendations covering training, exchanges, research, and the integration of women, are being tackled in a second pan-African project which is, in part, a response to the survey.

THE RESEARCH FINDINGS, IN BRIEF

Terms of reference

The survey covered eleven African countries: Benin, Burkina Faso, the Congo, Ghana, Kenya, Mali, Senegal, Chad, Togo, Zaire, and Zimbabwe. They were chosen to represent a cross-section of three variables: historical heritage, geographical location, and the existing radio communication models.

The study examined different radio broadcasting experiences, particularly in rural areas, and touched on the following points: the general environment of radio (legislative, social, economic, cultural and political); the history and objectives of radio; and the organization, programming, technical and financial situation of rural radio. Popular participation and the situation of women as professionals and as a target audience were a focal point of the survey.

Vertical vs. horizontal communication

Rural radio has existed in Africa since the early 1960s. Generally speaking, its objectives are almost identical from one country to another. Rural radio has a mandate for development, the broadcast of local culture, and conveying government development policies. It aims to increase production and agricultural productivity by developing knowledge; to organize dialogue between peasants and the authorities, as well as among the peasants themselves; and to further cultural heritage and traditions.

Rural radio is often the offshoot of national development plans. It serves government policies in the area of production, especially industrial agriculture. The experience of Burkina Faso provides a good example of this. It is a desert country with one of the lowest levels of education in Africa. Radio was used by the government as a tool for economic and social development in the early days of the newly created State. When rural radio was initiated in 1969, its purpose was to create the main support, and to be the key element in the mobilization of any government programme aimed at the welfare of the population.

Today, programmes may cover groundnut production based on segments recorded throughout the year, or how to go about obtaining credit from a financial institution. Educational programming on themes such as fish hatcheries and raising rabbits, emphasizes training peasants in specific tasks, allowing them to contribute to the production process.

Another of the research findings was that the efficiency of rural radio is often limited by its structure and a lack of peasant involvement in determining its programming. Programmes are often broadcast on a single radio network that sometimes does not reach the entire country.

Generally speaking, rural radio is integrated into the national (state) broadcasting structures. It may consist of local productions linked to national programming, as it does in Mali; it can be a department in itself, as in Senegal; or a State-owned enterprise, as in Zaire.

In Burkina Faso, rural radio was a service of the national broadcasting system until 1981, when it became a separate department. In Benin, rural radio eventually became a specialized division with relative autonomy in management. Today, this service falls under the authority of the Director of Broadcasting and, according to the AMARC/CIERRO research report:

> This situation generates many problems. There is often a lack of coordination between similar programming organizations and other national broadcasting structures, as well as overlaps and duplication in programming. As rural stations are not autonomous, they inherit the administrative, structural and financial problems of the structures which oversee them. (AMARC, 1990)

For a long time, this situation of dependence and guardianship left its mark on the training of rural radio workers, or the lack thereof. To be a communicator in national languages was not considered important by many people. The creation of CIERRO helped to change this mindset and improve the availability of training, at least in Francophone Africa; however, not enough rural radio workers have access to this training.

While the survey pointed to a low level of listener participation in planning and programming, a few experiences were identified in which rural associations participated at these levels. The experience of Burkina Faso, for example, with half a dozen local stations, has been largely positive due to popular involvement in all stages of the creation of the stations and continued participation in their programmes, which are thus truly able to reflect the concerns of local people.

A lack of systematic methods to measure the impact the programmes have on the population makes evaluating their effectiveness difficult. Where they exist, collective listening practices (through radio clubs, for example) provide for regular feedback from rural people. Other direct or indirect methods such as interviews and mail are also used to gather feedback.

It is possible to say that with the emphasis that has been put on national languages and local cultures, the people are more interested in rural radio. But has the objective of "liberating peasant speech," expressed by the directors, been reached? Far from it — even further when one considers the very limited place of women as both professionals within the stations and as an intended audience for the programming.

NEW RURAL RADIO MODELS

It is true that within the leadership of State radio broadcasting there are a few people who want to give more space to the voice of the people, either by way of new programmes, or by way of promoting local languages. Initiatives are being undertaken for a radio which is closer to the people (Benin and Zaire) and for rural radio independent of State radio broadcasting (Mali). In many countries professional associations and women's groups are intervening to ensure that local needs are taken into account when programmes are conceived.

Original experiences and actions have been identified — for example, Kayes Rural Radio in Mali, Radio Candip in Zaire, and local stations in Burkina Faso.[1]

Kayes Radio was developed as a result of the participation of two Italian NGOs: Terra Nueva and Gao, in the context of a larger development project in the Sahelian region.

The designers of the Kayes radio project recognized the fact that people are more likely to respond positively to development efforts when they feel as though they are a part of the process. The AMARC/CIERRO research report described this project:

> In the model adopted for Kayes radio, the rural population is considered the protagonist of development. The specific role of the radio is to reinforce the cultural self-identification of the population, to systematically confront technical and social knowledge, to broadcast the information necessary to support economic development initiatives, and to improve living conditions. (AMARC, 1990)

The Kayes radio's most important programmes deal with socio-cultural and economic sectors, health, and literacy. They are broadcast in local languages, keeping with Mali's strong oral tradition. The station is managed by the local population, and is currently working with four large villagers' associations. There are at least 402 villages are involved in the project.

> Each village chooses a producer, who is provided with portable recording equipment. The producer then decides on a theme for a programme, records the villagers' concerns, and the programme is put together based on villagers' feedback. (Cavazzani, 1990)

Radio Candip in Bunia, Zaire, was created in 1974. Its programmes encourage popular participation in local development, and offer solutions to the villagers' problems.

Programmes are produced in ten languages, with many segments devoted to women's issues. Major themes are defined for the year, based on villagers' concerns, expressed to the producers during local visits. One producer noted: "Visits (to the villages) allow us access to first-hand sources of information; our 'guide book' is the villager struggling for a better life."

Local rural stations in Burkina Faso have already made a valuable contribution to an overall participatory development project. Local radio, by giving peasants the ability to express themselves, serves as a crucial channel for the promotion of effective popular participation for development.

> Since rural radio began in Burkina Faso, people have been better able to discuss their ideas and objectives. Rural populations have built radio stations for themselves. Radio productions have to be created by the population. Producers have to be recruited from inside the population.

WHEN POLITICS GET MIXED IN

Popular movements demanding democratization and the demands of professional groups and development organizations have contributed to dramatic changes in the African media landscape in the past two years. Changes in the broadcast media have been slower and more difficult than in the printed press, since control over broadcasting ultimately rests in the hands of powers who continue to resist pluralism and the idea of popular participation. Nevertheless, there are a number of changes taking place.

Some national radio broadcasting structures have already allowed the inauguration of new stations. In Mali, Radio Bamakan began broadcasting in the capital in late 1991, as the second community station in Mali. It joined Kayes Rural Radio, which has existed independently for four years.

Mali's interim government tried to silence the new radio station in the early stages of its existence, but popular protests resulted in the granting of a temporary license to Radio Bamakan. A decree was passed legalizing the private media in early 1992; Radio Bamakan is now authorized to broadcast to the entire city, as is a new commercial station.

The station transmits 12 hours daily of volunteer-produced, educational and cultural programming in several national languages: Bambara, Peul, Solinké, Sarakolé, and French. Their purpose is to reflect the needs and concerns of the city's population.

Canal Arc-en-ciel, in Burkina Faso, has been broadcasting music and participatory programmes since December 31, 1991. One year earlier, Burkina Faso saw the emergence of a private station, Horizon FM. This was the first experience of its type in Francophone Africa. Decidedly commercial, the owners of Horizon are planning on starting a second station in the second largest city, in 1992. The creation of this last station is perhaps not as innocent as it seems.

A debate is beginning to take place around the issue of participatory radio vs. commercial radio. Democratizing the airwaves remains the task at hand — but what type of democratization, of liberalization? Is it enough to put the medium in the hands of groups with the means to establish commercial stations, or is it necessary to take steps to actively promote the participation of the entire population?

It seems that in light of the actual state of things, there is no room to oppose either of these experiences. Participatory radio has no choice but to think about more commercial concerns which will ensure its relative financial autonomy. As for commercial radio, one cannot forget that its survival depends on a political atmosphere which recognizes pluralism and promotes democracy. Thus, it has a vested interest in working toward upholding the structures which will promote these elements, and which must have a strong participatory component.

Another issue which warrants consideration is popular participation. Africans have expressed the need to clarify this concept on many levels. While many agree that rural radio can no longer be merely "radio for the people," but rather, "radio by and for the people," the practices that will ensure this must be defined by Africans, and not by exterior forces.

Various alternatives may be looked at with respect to participatory radio: the creation of tape libraries and listening clubs, and initiatives which will seek out the participation of grassroots organizations. Some priorities have already been established. Training and research, for example, are essential to the implementation of popular participation, and the integration of women as programme producers, and as a target audience, is imperative.

AN AFRICAN NETWORK

It seems essential for people involved in rural radio production to create a continuous current of information which can be done, in part through the exchange of experiences — both on a continent-wide level and with other southern regions such as Latin America and Asia.

This exchange could permit all of Africa to benefit from a range of experiences — for example, that of a project created by the Tanzanian Media Women's Association (TAMWA). This project involves a radio unit which uses participatory methodology to improve the condition of women. According to one organizer:

> One of TAMWA's aspirations is to produce news concerning women from their perspective, and to quantitatively and qualitatively accelerate our professional excellence...The alternative media and theatre for development — these are what TAMWA wishes to use, as its members have discovered that they are traditional, pertinent, and involve rural people.

These reflections, combined with recommendations from the survey, have led CIERRO and AMARC to initiate a second project: the establishment of a pan-African network of participatory radio producers.

The project will constitute an active forum where people involved in rural or community radio will be called upon to exchange ideas and experiences and to work in a coherent, complementary manner on issues of popular participation, research and training. Another of its basic tasks will be to develop models for legislation that would permit different types of radio to function in the new space being offered for communications in Africa today.

Democratization goes far beyond the adoption of multi-party systems. True democratization is that which allows people to determine their future and the type of development best-suited to them. Participatory radio is certainly one tool that is well-suited to implement this vision in Africa.

* * *

NOTES

1. For a fuller description of Radio Candip and the Kayes radio station, see chapters 4 and 12.

DOCUMENTARY SOURCE MATERIAL

AMARC (1991) *Proceedings of the Seminar: Participatory Communication, Community Radio and Development, Montréal, April 11 and 12, 1991*. AMARC, Montréal, Canada.
AMARC (1990) *Study on Rural and Local Radio in Africa. AMARC,* Montréal, Canada.
Cavassani, Ada (1990) "Une radio rurale à Kayes," *Cooperazione,* French edition, July 1990. Ministry of International Relations, Italy.

15

New Voices

Eduardo Valenzuela

Mexico's National Indigenous Institute (INI) has a network of cultural radio stations which provides a communication service for about 3.2 million people, most of whom are indigenous. The stations broadcast in 28 native languages and reach almost half of the First Nations groups in the country. They are located in the principal towns of the twelve ethnic regions where they operate; towns which in general have all necessary services and where indigenous people from the countryside come to buy and sell, take care of official business or make use of health care services. For one reason or another they have to come to town often and it is not unusual for them to visit the radio station while they are there, either to put up a notice, drop off a tune or simply say hello to the announcers.

This rather special experiment in communication began in 1979 when XEZV, The Voice of the Mountains, went on the air in Tlapa de Comonfort in the state of Guerrero.

The overall aims of the stations in the network are:

a) to help improve the living conditions of the target population;
b) to help strengthen the culture of the settlements and communities which fall within the stations' range;
c) to promote and strengthen indigenous organizations as a way of achieving the free development of native peoples.

The programming that seeks to fulfil these aims falls into five main categories: Educational, cultural, news, entertainment, and "notices."

Educational programmes are intended to improve the social well-being of the listener. The starting point for producing these programmes is always the real conditions in which indigenous people live, focusing on culture, natural resources, legal problems, health and so on.

There is no doubt that *cultural programmes* have the biggest impact on the population. These programmes broadcast the communities' major cultural expressions, such as music, story-telling, feast days, history, customs and traditions.

News bulletins keep the communities informed about the most important events. International and national news from NOTIMEX, the Mexican press agency, is carried. However, there is an emphasis on local news provided by several regionally-based community correspondent networks.

Entertainment programmes are primarily intended to increase listenership. These programmes and the stations' music programming conform to listeners' tastes and expectations. However, the stations don't play so-called commercial music.

"Notice boards" provide an important communication service for the communities. They are special time-slots during which personal messages or messages from various institutions and organizations are read. In areas where only very few households have telephones, these are often the most effective way of delivering personal messages to family members in the next town or letting the members of an organization know of an upcoming meeting.

The common experience of the broadcasters and listeners has been extremely important. Studies recently carried out indicate that there is a very high listenership. Local people listen to their radio station not just to hear messages in their own language, but also because they strongly identify with it. And how could it be otherwise since they hear their own voices and their own music on the radio, and their hopes and desires are expressed over the air. Indeed, the success of these radio stations is due precisely to the fact that there is community participation on nearly all levels. There are three main ways by which listeners are able to participate in the programming.

First, and most importantly, the staff of the stations is almost entirely native. They are professionals, trained in radio production, cultural research and journalism, but they can also identify with and understand the listeners' culture and reality because it is their own.

Secondly, indigenous organizations produce programmes "in situ" at Radio Production Centres located at various places within the broadcast area of the stations. These programmes are then sent to the stations which broadcast them complete and unedited.

Finally, the networks of community correspondents that were mentioned earlier supply local and regional news and are a valuable way of enabling organised listener participation.

The type of participation and the degree to which it contributes to cultural self-definition varies widely throughout the network. The Zapotecs in the mountains of Northern Oaxaca, for example, have reached levels of organization and productivity which are diametrically distinct from those of the Rarámuris in the Tarahynara Mountains in Chihuahua. Whereas, for the Zapotecs, radio is a vehicle for discussing the projects of their various organizations and their successes and failures, the Rarámuris see it as essential only as a means of interpersonal and community communication. For the latter, the medium has not yet realized its potential for contributing culturally and organizationally to the community.

Community participation, although it has been the central focus of all radio activity, is still far from consolidating itself and making all the links that are needed. Participation continues to be spontaneous and individual and a lot must be done to transform it into something that can connect with the dynamics of the indigenous movement. There is no doubt that this is a reflection of the level of development of native people's movements and the extent to which they are present on the national political scene.

NEW RADIO STATIONS: PARTICIPATION, MANAGEMENT AND RESEARCH

It has been noted that indigenous radio stations are an efficient means of communication and of strengthening native culture in Mexico. One indicator of this is the numerous requests for assistance received by the National Indigenous Institute (INI) from organizations and communities wanting to set up their own radio stations. Although the Institute's financial resources are limited, there is an ambitious plan to set up 14 new radio stations, bringing the total to 26 by 1994 and providing the service to almost all of the indigenous communities in the country.

INI's efforts are not only financial. A participatory project with the political implications that this one has, inevitably needs a strategy in line with the democratizing spirit of the medium. It is absolutely necessary to be able to count on broad participation and direction from the very beginning of the project until the station goes on air, from choosing the equipment to the design of the programme schedule. In order to ensure this participation and direction, we have designed a research plan aimed at involving the community in determining what their station will be like. This research is conducted in every community before a radio station is set up.

The research plan involves three separate branches, each with its own aims, methodology and techniques. The first is a socioeconomic investigation whose aim is to determine in general terms the social, political and cultural infrastructure of the region. The second branch of research looks at media use and the habits of future listeners. Finally there is a participatory research project designed to define jointly with the listeners the specific aims of the station, what it will broadcast and how community participation will be achieved.

Socioeconomic research

This branch of research seeks to collect a body of documentary information about the region in which the station will operate. These studies will be a point of reference about the geographical, topographical conditions in the region and its natural resources.

A second activity in this research branch is a study of the region's labour processes. A detailed understanding of these processes will later permit the development of programmes that will provide technical assistance to farmers, forestry workers, and others.

The distribution processes and their resultant political-social system are also analyzed. This level of research is directed at identifying the various political forces (parties, organizations, citizens groups) and their interaction with one another and with outside bodies.

The final part of this research branch looks at the most important aspects of the culture of the indigenous groups who will participate in the station. This brief cultural investigation is aimed at understanding the mechanism of cultural reproduction, acculturation and the methods of resistance adopted when faced with the influence of dominant cultures.

Media use

By means of a series of surveys and interviews, this branch of the research hopes to identify the uses the communities make of the various mass media. Do they listen to the radio? At what time? What are their favourite programmes and what do they like about them? How long do they listen? Who turns the receiver on? This gives us a body of information which will be very useful when drawing up the programme schedule.

To carry out the surveys and the interviews we use what we call community researchers — peasants, volunteers or people chosen by the community involved in the project. The results are amazing, for each interview session is a rich exchange of information between the researcher and the people being interviewed.

Participatory research

This is the backbone of the research. It is based on a series of what we call *Thinking Workshops* — meetings with organizations in which we talk and think about the role that the radio station will have in the future.

This branch of the research is concerned with establishing the channels and mechanisms for community participation as well as working with future listeners to define what the radio station will be like. At the same time as considering the communication needs of the settlements, radio committees and their respective representatives are being elected. In this way we are able to determine who the community correspondents will be, where the Production Centres will be located, and the interest of each group in doing particular programmes. This knowledge is essential as we plan the programming.

As a guide to this research and the Thinking Workshops, we came up with three basic questions from which the programming goals, content and methods will follow.

What will a radio station do for us?

What will we want to broadcast?

How will we participate in it?

The process is very simple and very accessible to the community. The answers to each question are written down in a big note pad, taking great care to write them down as literally as possible. For example:

> The radio station that we are going to get, we will use it to stop our customs from being lost and so the kids will know the words of the elders, that's the use we will make of it.

The answers which come out in these meetings are like the one above, offered by elder in Zongolica, Veracruz. In the region Cora-huchol-tepeh-huana-meicanera, in the states of Nayarit and Jalisco, we were amazed at the clarity of the answers. The governors of the indigenous communities got together (they are the representatives of the traditional forms of government) and presented a series of questions to the station. "Why are we going to broadcast our customs, if they are ours alone?" was one comment made by a governor. This gave rise to a long discussion amongst themselves in which they realized the importance of radio. This same discussion put conditions on broadcasting certain cultural forms: ritual music could only be broadcast at the time of the celebration of a particular ceremony and in a limited way; certain rituals, which are closed or only for initiates or *maracames,* cannot be recorded; recording of rituals must be done with the approval of the governors, and so on. In order to solve these and many other problems the Assembly of Indigenous Governors, the leaders of the producers' organizations, and the *maracames,* formed the Consultative Council of the Voice of the Four Nations, whose function will be to run and monitor the station. In this way channels for indigenous participation in radio were established.

It is clear that participatory research does not end with just consulting people; it requires a way of organising the information obtained and then presenting it to the participants. This on-going process makes possible a continual prioritizing of suggestions according to the aims and headings which were mentioned at the beginning of this article. Thus, community discussion continues right up to the point when titles are being chosen for the programmes.

* * *

PART IV: CULTURE

The age of the broadcast media has been an age marked by the homogenization of culture on a world scale and with the suppression of local and alternative cultures. The chapters in this section show how three community radio stations have been able to provide an alternative to this trend by contributing to the development of national identity in Martinique, to cultural diversity in France, and to the promotion of alternative cultural material in Canada.

16

Radio Asé Pléré An Nou Lité[1]: A weapon for liberation

Condensed and adapted from a text by Richard Chateau-Dégat

The French colonization of Martinique in the 1700s resulted in the genocide of the Indigenous Carib Amerindians and introduced a slave trade which brought tens of thousands of black Africans to Martinique. Caribs who did survive sought refuge in neighbouring islands, in particular Dominica. As a result, Martinique has a forced mix of Amerindian, African and European cultures and the Martiniquan people have been left struggling to find their identity. Slavery was abolished following the anti-slavery revolution of 1848. However, even now the island is subject to French colonial rule.

Since the 1970s, the struggle for independence has been gathering new strength. This movement, which had been marginal for many years, now influences the entire social and political fabric of Martinique. Radio Asé Pléré An Nou Lité is an integral part of this movement, and its creation has been essential to the Martiniquan people's struggle for identity and liberation.

THE NEED TO COMMUNICATE

The second half of the 1970s saw a strongly motivated movement beginning to address social and cultural problems in Martinique. This movement is active at a grassroots level. Workers, peasants and youth have created popular organizations to address their needs in the countryside and in the shantytowns of the capital, Fort de France. Literacy campaigns, education and training programmes, improvements in sanitation and roads, and education in politics and history have sharpened people's understanding of their shared experience. Martiniquan culture has been brought to life through open air popular theatre, and the revival of *bélé* (the foundation of Martiniquan music). All this served to turn around the thinking of a community whose identity had been exemplified by the popular saying *Komplo nèg sé komplo chyen* — blacks have no say.

This new momentum in Martiniquan society was completely ignored by the media. Newspapers, radio and television feigned blindness and remained silent about both cultural and social changes that were taking place. They did report on a strike among agricultural workers in 1974, but only after two workers were shot by the authorities. Even then coverage was minimal. Progressive organizations were denied the right to disseminate information about their efforts and activities. As a result, they were being denied a less tangible, but equally important function of the media, because the need to communicate is not simply a need to share knowledge, but also to have others recognize the value of what we accomplish and who we are. It was important that the critical events and experiences that were transforming so many lives be recognized by the media in order to take them from the margins and give them status and a global dimension.

More and more people and organizations understood the necessity of legitimizing and representing what appeared to be scattered "marginal" events. There needed to be "a voice for the voiceless." And so the idea of a popular radio station developed, Radio Asé Pléré An Nou Lité.

FROM IDEAS TO ACTION

Once the decision was made to establish a station, the problem of finances arose. Because these difficulties could only be resolved with the help of people who felt a strong need for a "radio of the people," the campaign to create the station became a test of the actual support that existed for it.

The project was illegal and therefore dangerous. Furthermore, it would depend on the support of the social class least able to afford it. Despite these barriers there was massive popular involvement on many levels. Everyone wanted to make a contribution, no matter how modest. Aside from financial support, people contributed time and knowledge to recover and recycle the materials used to construct offices and install equipment. A metal pylon was sanded, welded and repainted to carry the antenna. Some farm workers put in two full days of physical labour. The casting of the concrete platform for the pylon was done at night (to avoid detection), with fifty volunteers working until two in the morning. They attributed the success of their unauthorized initiative to the fact that they made use of "French efficiency" and "not having learned good manners in school."

The people had created a resource through which they could express who they were — real Martiniquans! *Radio pep la*, the people's radio, was born.

DIFFICULT BEGINNINGS

For more than two years, Radio Asé Pléré An Nou Lité led a precarious existence. Programmes lasted three hours daily for the first year, longer on weekends. It wasn't much, but apparently too much for the authorities. They did everything possible, short of using force, to prevent the experiment from succeeding, jamming our signal and repeatedly cutting off our electricity. This, along with technical problems — due to our inexperience, the quality of equipment, installation problems and so on — often caused interruptions that lasted up to several weeks. We had to change frequencies more than once when those we were using were given to new, legal stations. We had to move our office three times and during one period we were forced to physically defend our equipment. People would guard the studio and the transmitters day and night. However, despite the many attempts to defeat us, Radio Asé Pléré An Nou Lité survived and is now firmly established in the Martiniquan media landscape.

A POOR RADIO STATION

Since 1981, several dozen FM radio stations have been established in Martinique. Some struggle along without personnel or finances and with low broadcasting power, while others have the financial support of a municipality or are able to get sizeable advertising contracts because of their connections. At the top end of the scale are two or three large stations linked to French media giants. While Radio Asé Pléré An Nou Lité is a poor station whose existence relies on public support, it is one of the stations authorized to broadcast to the entire island of Martinique.

Radio Asé Pléré An Nou Lité has survived its ten-year existence without any government subsidies. Membership fees from the "Association for the Development of Grassroots Communication" (ADECOBA) make up one-third of our resources. This organization was created in 1989 to develop support for the radio. Other resources come through donations from supporters. These are both financial and material (office supplies, studio equipment, etc.). Advertising was introduced in 1990, coinciding with the hiring of our first salaried worker. Advertising revenue still makes up only a modest part of our budget, falling below our objectives. This is in part due to our lack of experience in the area, but the very nature of Radio Asé Pléré An Nou Lité, which never hesitates to go against the grain of dominant ideas, does offend some advertisers. Although our financial situation makes the need for some advertising inevitable, we will not accept advertising from simply anyone. Instead, we actively promote small local businesses and producers and steer clear of the big advertisers. This has obviously kept us poor.

GRASSROOTS COMMUNICATION

The fundamental reason for the creation of Radio Asé Pléré An Nou Lité was the need for communication at the grassroots level. Consequently, we have always made listener access to the airwaves a top priority. Radio Asé Pléré An Nou Lité is a kind of permanent, popular forum. Major issues are introduced on the air and debated by the listeners themselves. The discussions go on for as long as there are ideas and arguments. As station administrators, we find this very satisfying because we know who our listeners are. But it is even more satisfying for the listener who can use the station to actively participate in public life. Of course, we are happiest when the telephone becomes inadequate and we hear the front doorbell ring. At that point, the listeners create the programming, with the "official host" playing a facilitating role for the "de facto hosts" in the audience. The ultimate stage is when a listener becomes a volunteer host. For example, Man Sicot, a listener who phoned in regularly, is now hosting a new show that she proposed and developed: *Si jénés té sav..., si gran moun té pé* ("If the young only knew, if the old only could"). Public participation is the best way to ensure that the station deals with topics relevant to our audience. When listeners speak on the radio, they establish an equal rather than hierarchical relationship with it. They demystify the medium for themselves and for other listeners by taking advantage of the opportunity to disagree with an analysis or commentary, or to add to a news report, or to hear this being done by others.

Because Radio Asé Pléré An Nou Lité's ultimate objective is the national liberation of the Martiniquan people, part of our struggle involves informing, educating and training our people. For this reason we have emphasized studying history and understanding economic conditions, devoted time to union training and information on workers' rights, and have developed shows on education, ecology and international news.

Radio Asé Pléré An Nou Lité has worked steadily for the democratization of the airwaves and the right to freedom of expression. This work is based on open and democratic debate. We encourage the expression of opposing points of view without censorship, and offer everyone the opportunity to fully explain and argue their positions. For example, even though we did not share the same views as the CSTM (Martiniquan Workers Trade Union Association) we offered them a daily one-hour show with no obligations, financial or otherwise. We did the same for the Association for the Protection of the Martiniquan Patrimony (ASSAUPAMAR) despite our differences of opinion.

PROMOTING INDIGENOUS MARTINIQUAN CULTURE

The dominance of French culture in Martinique has repeatedly denied the existence of an indigenous culture. We have been raised in a society that believes that real culture is learned at school and must come from elsewhere. Radio Asé Pléré An Nou Lité has challenged this attitude by promoting two integral elements of our culture: the Creole language and *bélé* — the foundation of Martiniquan music.

Broadcasting that is done exclusively in French (as is the case with many Martiniquan radio stations) has served to ensure that access to the airwaves is restricted to educated elites who are comfortable with the language. Anyone who uses Creole or anything less than "perfect" French on the radio is ridiculed. By using Creole on air we overthrow the usual order of things and allow the majority to control communication. We believe that everyone should be able to communicate without constraint or repression. Our linguistic policy is that those who do not master French should be allowed to speak Creole, and those who do not speak Creole well should be able to express themselves in French.

Open-mindedness has also informed our policies on music. While an important effort has been made to rehabilitate and promote "bélé," Radio Asé Pléré An Nou Lité also continues to be the station most open to both local music and music from all over the world. We do however, strictly avoid promoting commercial music even though we have come under a lot of pressure to change this policy. No doubt, the absence of big hits, both local and international, has cost us listeners. But as a result we have a unique identity; we are the radio station for those who are fed up with the sameness of all the others.

The inevitable challenges and setbacks that we have experienced in the last ten years have strengthened us and reaffirmed the raison d'être of Radio Asé Pléré An Nou Lité. We must continue to learn in order that our people may move forward, and that Radio Asé Pléré An Nou Lité and the spirit of community radio may live on and develop.

* * *

NOTES

1. Asé Pléré An Nou Lité is Creole for "Enough crying, to our struggle."

17

Radio Gazelle: Multi-cultural radio in Marseille

by members of the Radio Gazelle team

Marseille is a cosmopolitan city located in the south of France. It is a Mediterranean port which has seen its share of immigrants and travellers. In the last two decades this city, the second largest in France, has experienced much economic hardship. Predictably, this economic slump provoked social and political tensions in the city, torn between a rich and tourist area in the south, and an industrial and working class district in the north. Despite a declining population, the unemployment levels reached record highs, 15% for the general population and 40% for those under the age of 25. The increasing poverty and the rise of the right on the political scene have caused a resurgence of racial conflict throughout the 1980s.

In the midst of this socio-economic scenario, Marseille experienced the birth of numerous stations that were part of the "free" radio movement. This movement began circa 1979, when "pirate" radio stations sprang up around the country. The enthusiasm for this type of radio grew in 1981 when the Socialists came to power and deregulated the airwaves, ending the State's monopoly. The free radio stations fulfilled an urgent need to give a voice to people who had been under-represented by the State broadcasters. A few months before the 1981 legalization, Radio Gazelle was born.

THE MAGHREB COMMUNITY RADIO[1]

Radio Gazelle was the initiative of a group of young people from the Maghreb, living in Marseille's northern district. Their initiative was based in a political desire to make their voices heard, to inform their community, and to ensure respect for its rights. Their actions enabled them to counter the cultural vacuum which had impeded the integration of this minority community with the rest of the population. With the aid of educators and activists, these youths began by broadcasting unbridled debates on weekends and at night. The broadcasts were accompanied by music from the Maghreb. They used a 100 watt transmitter and broadcast illegally.

One of the consequences of the Socialist Party's deregulation of the airwaves was that foreigners now had the right to form associations and own radio stations. Thus, Radio Gazelle was formally incorporated and became the principal activity of the Association Rencontrer Amitié. Today, Radio Gazelle is located at street level in the heart of the working class district, in its own building. The area is primarily inhabited by immigrant workers.

The name Radio Gazelle came by chance during one of the many meetings of the team. Nobody remembers exactly who came up with the name. One theory is that it was chosen because it has the same pronunciation in French and in Arabic.

TOWARD PLURALISM

Today, after over ten years, Radio Gazelle is firmly established. Initially, the station was known for its roots in the Maghreb community, then it gradually opened its doors to the various communities making up the Marseille cultural mosaic. This change did not occur without some heated debates. These discussions concluded with a decision to avoid conditions which ghettoize a community, and to open the station to other cultural communities. The decision to go forward with this project of de-compartmentalizing the airwaves was a result of regular contact between various ethnic groups in the same neighbourhood, as well an involvement in various debates on issues of common concern. It would have been hypocritical to fight for equality and for a pluralist France while maintaining an isolationist attitude towards our own radiophonic space. After much discussion, the term "multiculturalism" was added to the mandate of Radio Gazelle.

The redefined mandate was initially quite polemical, for each person understood multiculturalism in a way that is most convenient for them! Endless debates raged about the smallest details. Certain militants of

European origin left, claiming there was not enough Arabic music on the air. In another case, some atheists adamantly opposed special programming for Ramadan.[2] The diverse ideologies represented within the teams running Radio Gazelle erupted during these conflicts and created an explosive environment.

RAMADAN

While Radio Gazelle is not a religious station, it has always provided its listeners with the opportunity to express and live out their Muslim traditions in Marseille. One way this service takes form is through special programming during Ramadan. Every year, for over ten years, Radio Gazelle sets up a temporary schedule during Ramadan. Each day, starting at 6:00 pm, volunteer announcers call for the breaking of the fast. Special programming continues until two or three in the morning. This programming consists of religious music, radio plays, games, debates and interviews with spokespeople from the Muslim community of Marseille. There is also programming done in cooperation with radio stations in Algeria, Morocco, and Tunisia.

Ramadan is an important component of the activities at Radio Gazelle and our listenership increases five fold during this period — after all, in terms of number of adherents, Islam is France's second religion.

Religious programming did not appear at Radio Gazelle without ruffling some feathers. During the first Ramadan, the Maghreb team wanted to rearrange the schedule in order to satisfy the demands of their Muslim listeners during the celebration. This required substantial changes in the regular programming. Many of the regular programmers were vehemently opposed to allowing what they saw as temporary disruptions to affect their programmes. The issue affected the station and the relations between programmers for years, until in 1986, a vote by a General Assembly of the association made a definitive ruling on the issue.

RESOURCES

Radio Gazelle has 143 volunteer members, of which 42 are on-air announcers. These volunteers give not only their time but also contribute financially to the station and its programming. Indeed, Radio Gazelle has survived and grown thanks to the dedication of these volunteers, and their contribution is unmatched in real value by other, larger, financial contributions.

Notwithstanding the trials and tribulations they have had to face, the volunteer teams which have managed the station have succeeded in achieving the two principal goals the station had set: multi-ethnic representation and the preservation of the political independence of the station.

Radio Gazelle also receives some support from the French government, which assures it a certain basic stability. It does not receive any money from foreign governments. Of its total budget of 800,000 francs[3], one third comes from a fund operated by the Ministry of Communication. Another French government programme, the Fonds d'action sociale pour les travailleurs imigrés et leurs familles (Fund for social action for immigrant workers and their families) also provides a third. The remaining third comes from a grant from the city of Marseille, membership dues, advertising, and various other minor sources. With these funds Radio Gazelle operates 24 hours a day, 365 days a year.

The station broadcasts in 13 languages, although Maghreb and oriental Arabic still account for 30% of the programming. The rest of the time is shared by European languages (French, Spanish, Portuguese, Greek and Italian), African languages (Comoran, Malagash, Kabyle and Wolof), Creole and Armenian. Radio Gazelle is indeed a multicultural forum which represents up to twenty cultural communities.

The wide spectrum of Radio Gazelle's programming takes various forms. The news and information magazine programmes provide analysis of issues concerning immigrants. The various cultural programmes broadcast news and developments of the life of the community and encourage communication amongst various communities. In order to further facilitate the expression of its listeners, Radio Gazelle dedicates a portion of its programming to open-line shows. To complement its information and educational programmes, the station also offers various kinds of entertainment programmes that can be enjoyed by all of its listeners. In this category are: comedy shows, cultural and sports magazines, and serials. Finally, in addition to all this, we feature music from all corners of the world.

Radio Gazelle has won its place amongst the various communities of Marseille. It has become a permanent part of the community's life, so much so that during the events in Algeria in 1988, during the Gulf War, and during the troubles in Madagascar, Radio Gazelle gave a voice to various militants from associations defending human rights and representing various liberation movements.

It is not always easy to maintain a progressive political stance when one is of foreign origin and living in France, where the Muslim communities tend to be regarded either as a potential "Fifth Column" or as scapegoats. If Radio Gazelle accomplishes this difficult task it is, in part, thanks to innumerable French sympathizers — friends who aid and defend immigrants. It is also thanks to members of the station who after many arduous years have not relented and still energetically defend human rights and equality, and tenaciously support the causes of the Third World and of liberation movements. All this while having to fight against the increasing harassment of the French extreme right. This speaks volumes for the integrity of Radio Gazelle and its role as a tool of social change.

* * *

NOTES

1. Maghreb is a region in north Africa composed of Algeria, Morocco and Tunisia.
2. Ramadan is the ninth month of the Muslim year, a period of daily fasting from sunrise to sunset.
3. Approximately US$200,000.

18

Offbeat, In-Step: Vancouver Co-operative Radio

Dorothy Kidd

Co-op Radio is housed in a old stone building in Vancouver's Pigeon Park, the only public open space for blocks around. It used to be right in the midst of the city's centre but the commercial district has since moved west, leaving Pigeon Park on the margins. And what was once a well-appointed square in front of a prestigious bank is now used by people without money or resources, who are often homeless as well. The park is one of the clearest signs in the city of the widening gap between business development and the city's poor.

Inside Co-op's door, the sounds of the street follow you all the way up three long flights of marble stairs to the broadcast studios. The tall windows are not sound-proofed and the traffic noise punctuates every broadcast. There's a "honnk whoosh" picked up every time the microphones go on, and you learn either to ignore the fire and ambulance sirens, or to make them part of the patter.

Listening in the car or at home, you would never mistake 102.7 FM for the flat, carefully modulated voices that arise from the sound-proofed studios at the Canadian Broadcasting Corporation (CBC), Canada's State-funded service. When Co-op Radio first began, it modelled itself on the public access broadcasting of the heyday of the CBC, an era which gave *Citizen's Forum* and *Farm Forum* to the world. Early Co-op programmers used a CBC-like format of interview-based shows, although their specialty was the presentation of unedited versions of public meetings and events. The Co-op pioneers defined their work as "alternative," amplifying opinions and voices which were seldom heard in the mainstream. For many of them, "alternative" also meant opposition to the status quo.

Ironically some of those early Co-op broadcasters went on to work at the CBC, where "public" has come to mean a centralized State service, and where budget cuts have reduced the staff to a small core of professional broadcasters. Co-op Radio, by contrast, despite continual financial concerns, and while keeping many of the CBC current affairs formats, also widened its notions of "public" and "alternative" to include programming by and for many of the city's special interest and cultural groups.

WE'RE ALL FANS

One of the first challenges to the original "alternative" approach came from a group of young men active in the local music scene. Peter Thompson has been active in music programming since those heady days in the mid 1970s:

> There was nobody else at the station who wanted music. So it was up to a few obsessed people with pretty highly developed visions to convince the station that in fact there should be a place for music. Once we went on the air, we didn't start with very many music shows, but they were consistently the best shows.
>
> Partly it was the material that was played, partly it was the passion of the people involved and partly it was the format. The presentation of music here is more distinctly different from mainstream or even college presentation than our current affairs is from mainstream or even college presentation. In North America, the core of radio programming is music. The music on commercial radio is treated like any other commodity that the station is advertising, and as stations compete for declining advertising dollars, they target their music programming to narrow bands of young consumers. The result is fewer kinds of music, and fewer selections. Combine that with a trend towards deregulation in Canada, and it is no wonder that few radio stations in Vancouver play anything but pop. In contrast to the commercial stations' trend to "narrowcasting" as they shed unprofitable programming, Co-op Radio has broadened its programming to include communities no longer served by mainstream radio, a policy of "specialcasting." The station

> brings together programmers who present music from all over the world, putting it into a historical and social context.

Janie Newton Moss co-produces a show on Sunday afternoons called *Black Tracks* which is devoted to African-American popular music.

> Just take something like Black music. If you're listening to it on mainstream radio you're going to get the most commercial, the least interesting end of the spectrum. You're going to get the records that sell.

Jim Stewart works on a Friday late-night show called *Offbeat*:

> What you're doing is presenting the foundations of something before it's made its way through the ringer of the music industry.

Janie again:

> We're all fans...it comes from a very obsessional place, which can be true of people involved in political change as well.

PLAYING MUSIC FOR FRIENDS IN YOUR LIVING ROOM

Gary Cristall's first aim was to "do radio as if you're playing music for friends in your living room." In 1977, he and Vinny Mohr started playing music from Latin America in a show they called Tres Culturas, to reflect its Indigenous, African and Spanish origins. At that time, there was nowhere else on the dial that you could hear Latin American music.

> I liked playing it for people. We were able to introduce a lot of people to a lot of stuff that I don't think they'd hear otherwise. Amparo Ochoa, Chavela Vargas, some of the new song people...We thought it was a way of introducing a lot of other people to something we believed in.

At the same time, he helped start the Vancouver Folk Music Festival. Through this work, he began receiving demo tapes from musicians around the world and he and Vinny began a show called Music of the World, their aim often unapologetically political.

> I certainly regard the work I do with music as political work. Especially when you're working with music that's outside the mainstream, where every bit of it communicates ideas. It may be preaching to the converted, but I've never thought that preaching to the converted was wrong...
>
> There are people out there who think they are alone in what they think. Sometimes when they hear the ideas that go around in their heads — sort of inarticulate feelings — articulated by great artists, that encourages people, in the sense of giving people a sense they're not alone, reinforcing the ideas they have.
>
> Certainly in the women's movement, in the peace movement, the environmental movement, the trade union movement, music has played a big role. Very few people can remember speeches that they have heard at political events, but most of them can remember songs they have heard. And I think that's always a kind of litmus test of the importance of music in political activity.

Gary and Vinny were unusual among those early music programmers. Most of the others would have defined their shows as "alternative" rather than "political." While mostly young and white, their musical interests were very eclectic. Their shows tried to provide an historical and social context, whether it was for rock and roll, rhythm and blues, country, folk, gospel, or jazz.

They also recorded local bands live at a number of the clubs in Vancouver or brought them in to play live in the studio. Peter Thompson:

> This is pre-punk, this is pre-people putting out their own records and tapes. So we had to record the music if we wanted to play it.

Those live shows tapered off as clubs stopped hiring musicians in favour of piping in taped music, and as that generation of programmers started getting tired of spending long hours dragging equipment up all those stairs. Many of them still present shows at the station. Many have also put their energy into building a number of alternate music enterprises, putting on concerts and festivals, or producing music shows for the CBC. Their years and breadth of experience brings a real strength to the station's programming. Their widening range of contacts also means that they can feature music that is either ahead of the record stores, or unavailable on the commercial market.

THE NEXT GENERATION(S)

In the ensuing years, newer generations, and very different subcultures and communities have started music programmes. The list is long — from reggae, to punk, to classical, to Hong Kong pop, Jewish traditional music, women's music and aboriginal music. A lot more women and people of colour have become involved in creating their own shows and participating in a few of the established ones.

For many of these new groups, there is still the need to record live material; it is still the case that women make up 10% of the pop charts and, except for rap artists, there are few recordings of Aboriginal people or people of colour. From 1985-1991, Ina Dennekamp produced a show called *Women of Note*, which focused on the work of women composers.

> It was fantastic to have the musicians come down to the studio, set up the band and talk about what they're doing. They were grateful to Co-op Radio to have this opportunity. They're in there making music and I'm just feeling wonderful about meeting the people on the other side of the music.

Kerry Charnley features the work of First Nations artists in her show on Friday nights called *When Spirit Whispers*. There are few artists recorded, so she collects tapes that other artists have produced themselves, or does her own recording of performances and events.

> Part of why we started doing *When Spirit Whispers* was as an educational thing, to show people that there's more than Plains drumming as far as Native music goes. There's rap and there's jazz and there's classical...
>
> It seems that there's a lot of public affairs programming (about Native issues), but there wasn't any musical or art programming. And that's a big part of any culture. So we thought it would be really important to get the music and the words out from Native people, so that the artists would have a forum, have a voice through the radio and thereby get the philosophy within Native cultures, Native nations out there.

That sense of music as a way to bridge gaps strikes a common chord among many programmers. Rani Gill thinks that "music can be really subversive." In a show called *49th and Main,* directed to the Indo-Canadian community, she plays a wide variety of classical Indian music and contemporary bangra, Punjabi dance music that mixes traditional forms with western instrumentation. While bangra's popularity began in England, it is also closely tied with the identity of the second and third generations of the community here.

> It's a way of drawing them in. That's their music. That's what they identify with.

"IT'S KIND OF LIKE A TUPPERWARE PARTY"

Some of us in the North American women's movement a generation earlier, used music in much the same way. Music was magic, in its capacity to articulate both voice and passion, and mix it with pleasure and collective cohesiveness. Connie Kuhns was the first woman to test that out at the station with her show *Ruby Music.*

> The whole idea of tying women's music and radio together was to create revolution. Those were the words we used at the time...I knew that this music was really really important. I'd been to enough concerts to watch women transformed, thousands of them at a time. One thing that was really lacking was any sort of women's musical perspective at Co-op Radio.

She originally conceived of her show as a kind of "consciousness raising," from the 1970s feminist idea of the "personal as political," where every story can be put into context. She laughingly described it as "kind of like a Tupperware party, getting together for the day to day."

Because of the work of Chris Williamson, Holly Near, Alix Dobkin and Meg Christian, American feminist music that had been so important to her, Connie originally planned to feature only those recordings from the American women's movement labels.

> From my own lack of musical history, I didn't fully appreciate what women had done before me — I thought women's music began in

> 1973. My eyes were opened as I began to look at the music of my youth, of my teenage years, and instead of wondering why women weren't doing certain kinds of music, I was wondering why I wasn't ever told what they did.
>
> At the time I saw (my audience) as the women's community, but within two years I had a lot of others, men and women who hadn't been involved in the community at all, listening.
>
> They started writing and calling me. And then the male music programmers eventually came around and they were gracious enough to admit they were prejudiced. Once they came around I knew I was onto something, and it's been a pretty broad-based audience ever since.

Connie still gets a strong reaction from her listeners for her mixture of contemporary song and story.

> I met a woman a couple of years ago who had found her way out of her previous life by reading *Kinesis* (a local feminist publication) and listening to *Ruby Music.* When she had had enough, she came to the city.
>
> Another woman wrote and said that when she first started listening to my show, she would get mad at me all the time. Part of the reason (was that) she was getting mad at herself, because she couldn't believe that she was as old as she was and didn't know that women had accomplished so much.

Connie attributes the impact of her show to the beauty and power of women's music, and also to the nature of radio.

> Radio is so personal and so private. You get a chance to reach people without embarrassing them, or without making them have to take a stand. They can sit at home and hear something and feel something and there's no one around to see, and then they can take it from there.

ISOLATING WOMEN'S MUSIC

In the last ten years, Co-op Radio has widened its schedule to include music from women and from other disempowered groups in Canada and the rest of the world. However, as a listener and programmer, this change doesn't always seem consistent throughout the schedule. The tendency to compartmentalize does not go unnoticed by women programmers.

As Connie Kuhns says:

> More women are doing music shows, and not just women's music but all kinds of shows. But I don't know that music shows produced by men are that conscious, except on special occasions, to play music by women...I think it's still mostly women's work that's doing it.

Like Connie, Ina Dennekamp's *Women of Note* had a varied listenership of both women and men, classical music lovers and those willing to experiment with the unfamiliar. Ina:

> I presented the material as though it had every right to be anywhere. I'm a real believer in making feminist inroads into people's lives and experiences in many different ways. Radio gives you the opportunity to present material that is different or unusual or perhaps challenging to people in a way they can hear it. Whether I dealt with feminist issues, or lesbian issues, or music by lesbians, it would be presented as such, but it would be done in the context of — this deserves to be heard anywhere. It's feminist by definition.

Nevertheless Ina was affected by the tendency in the station to isolate women's issues.

> There's a danger of having a "woman and anything" program. It tends to be ghettoized. The station says, "well now, the 'woman and whatever issue' is taken care of, because there's Ina's program over there," which is exactly opposite to the original intent. Here I am gathering up all this information, but still it is separate from and aside from mainstream Co-op even, to say nothing of mainstream life anywhere else.

During the 1980s women programmers such as Ina, Connie, Jane, myself and many others began to encourage other women and men to do programming about women, at least during the week of March 8, for International Women's Day.

> The intention was that all programmers take up the idea that women's issues are not particular to women, that it is a global problem, that it is a community problem. It's still a problem. There simply wasn't enough of that. The integration simply hasn't taken place — that was always the danger in my mind of having a ghettoized program.

FUTURE TRENDS

We have a special challenge on community radio stations like Co-op Radio, whose traditional approach to programming has been the "patchwork quilt" of special interest publics and shows. The station's Board and Programme Committee is working towards creating an integrated overall vision which will allow for special needs and interests, by encouraging the participation of new people and the development of new shows.

Music programmers have demonstrated a number of strategies on their own. Connie makes sure to bring in younger women to guest host and tell their own musical stories from time to time and a few of the other established shows have made a point of integrating women into their programme staff. The newer shows have presented another way to see the problem and resolution.

One of Kerry's dreams is to produce programming from the Musqeam and Squamish reserves. Another is to bring in more elders "because they have a lot of knowledge and experience in the culture, philosophy and values, and also have a real way with words."

Knowing that much of her audience is not aboriginal, she wants to produce a bilingual language spot in Salish and English, "so people would get familiar with the sound of the Salish language." It sounds similar to what Rani Gill of *49th and Main* has suggested.

> That's what people should be doing more of, to stretch people's listening. Interviews have a place, not just music, because using voices is music. I want people to be listening to marginalized voices and languages. You don't need to understand a language. You can listen to the rhythms of the breath, the tonality of the voices and how they intersect. I want to use voices as a form of music and mix them, both for those who know the language and those who don't. That's what Co-op Radio is supposed to be about, bringing voices in from the margins.

Walking through Pigeon Park this morning you can look up into the tall trees that stand by the windows of the studio. Two of the station's pioneers, Howard Broomfield and Hildi Westerkamp created music by hanging their mikes out onto those trees to bring the voices in. Since those days of environmental music programming, Co-op Radio has opened up the airwaves to more closely represent Vancouver's population, and especially to those who are denied access elsewhere by virtue of their race, sex, class or politics. There's a lot more room for institutional changes but a creative renewal is beginning, revamping and recycling older ideas of music and of formats to better fit the sounds of today's streets.

* * *

PART V: BEGINNINGS

The previous sections have focused on the practice of community radio and the supportive role that it plays in social movements. We have also seen a number of examples of the hostility that community radio projects have received from institutions resistant to those same social movements and their visions for society. Getting on air in the face of this hostility is the first hurdle that any community radio must overcome.

The chapters in this final section of the book look at some of the strategies used by community radio broadcasters in their efforts to get on the air. The experiences presented in this section share two common characteristics: They began as alternatives to legal community radio, and they were the beginnings of campaigns for legal and viable community radio.

19

The New Wave: The emergence of low-power radio in Argentina

Condensed and adapted from a text by Arturo E. Bregaglio and Sergio Tagle

Argentina used to be considered a rich country. However, as the end of the twentieth century approaches, it is undergoing one of the worst crises in its history. Many Argentineans thought that when democracy returned in 1983, economic prosperity would also return. However, after nearly three years of Carlos Menem's Peronist government, its neoliberal economic policies have only worsened the situation.

Indiscriminate privatisation, declining production, lack of investment and a virtual end to the economic role of the State, have all served to deepen the crisis on both the social and economic level. There has been a dramatic increase in poverty and unemployment, wealth is becoming concentrated in fewer hands. Urban crime, apathy and hopelessness are on the rise. Traditional roles, both in the family and in society, are breaking down. The union movement has suffered enormous setbacks; increased unemployment coupled with the Menem government's anti-union policies have left workers demoralised and unprotected. There is disenchantment with traditional political parties and consequently participation in the political process is declining. Old political organisations are becoming fragmented. A new culture based on unemployment and the informal or underground economy is being created. Unlike a culture based on the dignity of labour, this culture tends to degrade, marginalise and destroy any hope for the future.

It is against this background of crisis and disintegration that we shall examine the emergence of low-power radio stations in Argentina, the legal framework in which they exist, and Radio FM Sur, one example of this new wave of broadcasters.

SOMETHING NEW UNDER THE SUN

Small FM radio stations began to crop up all over Argentina as early as 1986. Over 2,000 of them, broadcasting programmes dealing with neighbourhood problems and other matters of local interest sprang up. They were often started by small groups of people who wanted to democratize communications and give a voice to all of those who had been silenced by years of military dictatorship. Neither legal nor illegal, the stations operated in a regulatory vacuum that existed because of the lack of any broadcast legislation covering the FM band. This low-power radio movement quickly gained popularity within communities, and just as quickly discovered enemies in a mainstream communications industry which feared that the competition would result in declining profits.

In September 1986, the Asociación de Radiodifusoras Privadas (ARPA, the Association of Private Radio Stations) organised a national meeting of commercial broadcasters. One of the outcomes of this meeting was the so-called *Mar del Plata Declaration.* Among other things, this declaration "reaffirms the need for absolute respect for the Constitution and the Law, and thus the elimination of clandestine radio stations as well as the suppression of all activities which undermine the legal order." Later, ARPA gave COMFER (Comité Federal de Radiodifusión/Federal Broadcasting Committee, the government body charged with regulating broadcasting) a list of 60 "clandestine" radio stations they wanted closed down and their equipment seized. (ARPA and other institutions insisted on referring to the unlicensed stations as clandestine, despite the fact that they operated openly). COMFER response to this and other pressure was inconsistent. At times they would close stations, but at other times they seemed content with merely issuing general warnings against unlicensed broadcasts.

Meanwhile, ownership of the media, including television, the press, and radio, was becoming increasingly concentrated in the hands of a few large corporations. In response to this, some provinces passed new broadcast laws, making use of an article in the Constitution which allows states to "promote activities of interest" in their territories. Several municipal radio stations, serving the needs of the local population, sprang up in

Patagonia, near the Chilean border. These have been on the air ever since, despite several attempts by the border police to close them down.

Some people have welcomed the development of community radio, others are violently opposed. In August 1987, while visiting Puerto Madryn, Senator Hipólito Solari Yrigoyen welcomed "the presence of the new Radio Libre station because it ends the monopoly of LU 17." In Córdoba, on the other hand, Pedro Sánchez, COMFER's Standardization Officer, declared: "My principal wish is that Argentina will be rid of this plague of underground radio stations."

As the number of underground radio stations increased, so did the pressure from certain economic and political sectors which wanted them closed down. The Alfonsin government proposed a draft Broadcasting Law which it hoped would put an end to all the contradictions. This proposed law would allow cooperatives, unions, nongovernmental organisations and social organisations to operate radio and television stations. The Christian Democrats presented their own draft Broadcasting Bills.

In 1987 the Asociación de Radios Comunitarias (ARCO) was founded in response to all the legal uncertainty. It represented various low-powered radio stations and provided them with information about legislative activity and possible closures. The legislation being proposed by the government required that radio stations broadcast with a minimum of 1,000 watts of power. The cost of such a station was beyond the reach of existing stations. In May 1988, another group of radio stations founded the Asociación de Radiofusoras Libres Argentinas (Association of Free Argentinean Radio). The 250 radio stations that were members of this association sent a letter to members of parliament in which they said that "free or underground radios are an essential form of social expression and they make it possible to broadcast information relevant to the small communities where they exist."

There was public support for the radio stations and at the *III Jornadas de Comunicación Social* (Third Gathering on Social Communication) in 1988 panellists debated the question of community access and participation in the new stations. One of the speakers focused the debate effectively:

> Faced with the false contradiction between State owned media and privately owned media driven by the pure logic of profit, there is a need to legislate for a third type of media,

which is socially owned and where the voices of unions, ethnic and religious minorities and other organizations can be heard.

While the parliamentary debates on the broadcasting issue dragged on, the opponents of community radio began to act. ARPA, the association representing private stations, broadcast prime time radio and television ads which accused the government of "judicial passivity and ineffective policy." A few months later, ARPA started legal proceedings against the Secretary of State for National Communication, "for not acting against clandestine radio stations." Pedro Sanchez, COMFER's Standardisation Officer, was another opponent of the proposed law. In May 1988 he said the existence of over 400 clandestine radio stations and television repeater stations constituted "acts of institutional subversion." More pressure was brought to bear on the president, Alfonsin, by The International Broadcasting Association. Its Board of Directors sent a telegram to Alfonsin expressing concern about the situation in Argentina, accusing the government of exacerbating the situation by its behaviour, and criticising "legal and administrative passivity which has allowed the proliferation of clandestine radio and television stations."

At the height of the debate, representatives of the government and of the community radio association, ARCO, met for the first time. The meeting did not clarify the legal situation of the over 2,000 stations and they remained neither legal nor illegal.

In 1990 a presidential decree required all unlicensed stations to register with the government. Since then, intimidation, closures, and equipment confiscations have taken place in every province in the country. In May 1991, Fernando Enrique Paz, the president of the Communications Commission of the Argentinean parliament and a member of the government party, criticized his own government's actions, saying they "have the effect of ordering the closure of all the functioning FM radio stations."

During the campaign for the 1991 elections, threats to close down radio stations and seize their equipment suddenly ceased as aspiring politicians found them invaluable for reaching the electorate. It remains to be seen if this sensitivity to the population's needs will continue now that the elections are over. Today, stations of all shapes and sizes, representing every shade of ideology and opinion can be found on the Argentinean FM band.

FM SUR IN THE STREETS

FM Sur (South FM) is one of those stations. Born December 10, 1988, it owes its existence to the confused legal situation and to the efforts of the various groups who came together to set it up, including professional broadcasters who wanted to use their skills to help the community and CEOPAL (Centro de Comini-cación Popular y Asesoramiento Legal/Popular Communication and Legal Counselling Centre), a non-governmental organization.

FM Sur's home is in Villa el Libertador, a poor neighbourhood of more than 50,000 in Córdoba, Argentina's second largest city. The community is typical of many shanty towns in Argentina. Until a few years ago, only two stations were heard in the neighbourhood: LV2 and LV3, the most successful commercial radios in the province. Today, these stations still have the most listeners, but many people have switched to local FM stations not covered by current legislation. In Villa el Libertador people listen to FM Sur.

What they hear is community radio, radio that answers their needs. Listeners can send messages of all kinds to each other. Small store owners take out ads. There are programmes giving health information and neighbourhood leaders go on air to discuss problems, berate local government and announce upcoming meetings. Music of many genres livens the airwaves. Radio has become a constant companion.

> Radio is the only medium which can enter into everyday life...A medium that its listeners will basically define as company; a medium that far from calling for any effort or interrupting their life, adapts itself to its listeners.

We do not know exactly how many people listen to FM Sur. The station gets over 500 messages per day and many more than that must listen. We do know that FM Sur has created a close emotional link with its listeners and that it gives them a sense of belonging. This observation is based on the letters and messages sent to the station: *Don't ever change; In my book, you get a rating of ten; You are the best radio station; I consider you my best friends; I like you very much; Thanks for making housework more bearable.*

Attendance at the party we held on our third birthday also showed how popular we have become. We invited people "to celebrate three years of being together with you and your family, three years of sharing experiences in Córdoba's neighbourhoods." There was no well-known musical group, just local musicians, but more than 1,500 people came. Considering the current political and cultural mood in Argentina, that is a lot of people.

A poem written by one of our listeners expressed the way people feel about FM Sur:

Words from my Neighbourhood
Carlos Garcia

Like a distant murmur
shy, emotional
a voice crossed space
and came to my radio...
It was crazy
turned the whole neighbourhood upside down
90.1 FM Sur
began to beam.
Now I can listen
to the voice of the people
of the poor
of friends and acquaintances.
December 10, 1988
is the unforgettable date
that with heartfelt solidarity
our radio began
The voice of the voiceless
because it belongs to the community
90.1 F M SUR
you are...
the voice of my neighbourhood

TRAINING AT FM SUR

What were we trying to do with FM Sur? We wanted to create a radio station listened to by the residents of this neighbourhood: one that becomes part of their daily lives; that has the potential to develop a political educational strategy; that answers to popular tastes while offering alternatives; that lets people express themselves on local as well as national issues and gives them a reference point from which to create a popular understanding of the world; that creates a place where those trying to create a popular urban movement in Córdoba can speak; that creates a space in which the popular sectors can talk to, negotiate with, agree with or confront authorities; and, finally, we wanted it to be participatory radio. This latter required us to have a thorough training programme, giving volunteer community members the skills and confidence they needed in order to produce their own programmes.

Our strategy is based in the practices of popular education, tailored to the interests, problems and wishes of each person. It includes theatre workshops that provide the skills necessary for production of radio sociodramas, communication workshops in schools, and training for correspondents from community organizations or from other neighbourhoods. We also spread the word and get feedback from the *Friends of FM Sur Club,* where the most active listeners meet, discuss, take part in auditions, organize dances, concerts and sporting events, and support campaigns for neighbourhood demands.

Throughout our three year history we have attempted to find a suitable training model. The models we have tried were usually influenced by what we thought about popular communications at the time.

At first we talked about participation. All we meant by this was opening up the mikes to the popular sectors. Later we decided that this was not enough. If we wanted more listeners, we had to produce *good* programmes. So we emphasised content and radio skills so we could produce high quality radio programmes. This was not enough either. We had not understood that often those who listen to radio are looking not so much for technical perfection or for good content but rather for something they can identify with, something that relates to their daily lives.

Now we try to think about those we are communicating with, their culture, their way of expressing themselves and their desire to listen to us. We believe that it is not the class origins of those behind the mike, nor the ideological correctness, nor the technical quality of the programmes that defines popular communication.

We believe that popular communication is more adequately defined as "a series of practices in which new communications actors — workers, peasants, the unemployed, women in all kinds of occupations, indigenous people, jacks of all trades, illiterate people, all the residents of the shanty towns — become visible to themselves and to society in a way which, although precarious and contradictory, is as distinct and significant as their own lives and cultures and the social movements that they create and which represent them."

* * *

NOTES

1. Mata, Marita. "Todas las voces." Cuadernos Barriales No. 8

20

Radio Stalin to Radio One: The first independent station in Czechoslovakia

Stanislav Perkner and Barbara Kent

The story of the first independent radio station in Czechoslovakia starts in November 1989, when the *Velvet Revolution* ended the Communist Party's domination of Czechoslovakia. Ever since the country's first radio stations were established in the mid-1920s, the medium had been dominated by the government. In the period between the two World Wars, broadcasting was the responsibility of a joint-ownership company, with the government holding the majority of shares. In 1948 this joint-ownership company was replaced with a State monopoly. The only exception to more than forty years of de facto control by the Communist Party's Central Committee was a few weeks of free broadcasting in 1968, the year of the invasion by Soviet troops.

There had never been an opportunity for the development of alternative radio stations and by November 1989, the official radio network paid little attention to listeners' needs, tastes and interests.

The political changes of 1989 were accompanied by efforts to break the State's broadcasting monopoly. The pioneering role in these efforts was played by a group of young people, mostly students, led by a sound technician, Vladimir Vintr, the current general manager of Prague's Radio One.

Breaking this monopoly was not going to be easy. In addition to the common problems arising from a lack of money and equipment, would-be independent broadcasters in Czechoslovakia had to cope with the lack of any legal status for their activities. Until recently, no one would have imagined that alternative broadcasting systems would one day appear. The law gave Czechoslovak Radio the exclusive right to broadcast and the government was historically more concerned with jamming foreign broadcasters like the Voice of America, Radio Free Europe, Deutschlandfunk and Vatican Radio, than it was with encouraging new voices.

The Velvet Revolution opened the doors to change for the State radio. News departments took up this option and adapted to their new role but music departments were reluctant. Young people were eager for a radio station that would provide them with rock music and other alternative genres. Restrictions that had limited this music were removed after November 1989, but music programming continued in essentially the same format.

WE WERE FIRST

The State radio's refusal to meet demands for a different type of programming contributed to a sense of frustration. Vladimir Vintr described what happened next.

> Our group of radio enthusiasts decided to take action. The father of one member of the group offered to let us use some basic broadcasting and studio equipment he had received from friends in Paris in the spring of 1990. The transmitter was strong enough to cover the city of Prague and its environs. We did not intend to break the law, and therefore we officially asked the radio communications office for a temporary license. We were promised two FM frequencies, but we did not receive a license because of the legal vacuum.

During this time, the government was deluged by requests from dozens of other applicants, both Czechoslovak and foreign. A new broadcasting law, which would provide a solution to the problem, was not forthcoming and the continual delays convinced any and all interested parties that something had to be done. Even a full year after the revolution, bureaucracy blocked the needed solutions.

This inertia contrasted with other creative activities, especially in the field of fine arts. For example, the Linhart's Foundation acted to promote alternative presentations in the arts. The Foundation had been established in 1987 by a group of Prague architects, but legally it was unable to present its creations until after November 1989.

In October 1990 the Foundation lent its support to a festival of independent culture, the *Totalitarian Zone*. One hundred and fifty artists came from some twenty countries to take part in the festival, organized in a very bizarre place — the basement rooms of the razed monument of Joseph Stalin in Prague. The monument had been demolished in 1962, but its three basement floors still kept the warehouse smell of dirty, dusty, moist and dank air. This absurd scene suited a *Totalitarian Zone.*

Vintr's radio group, still trying to get a licence, was invited to take part in the "happening" — a continuous party lasting day and night and well attended.

> Our broadcasts started Friday, October 19, at six p.m., and continued until Sunday. We offered music, and covered Festival events continuously on 92.6 FM, a frequency which we knew from previous negotiations with radio communications administrators did not interfere with other Prague stations. Of course, we knew that our broadcasting was pirate, the first in Czechoslovakia. But we also believed that it was the only way to provoke action from the decision-makers. We operated from the bizarre location of the former Stalin monument; that's why we called ourselves Radio Stalin.
>
> We knew immediately from the heavy telephone response that we had found the solution. Some of the listeners were shocked by our name, but that had been our intention: to appeal to the interest of public participation. The absurdities associated with 'underground activities' allowed us to use an 'absurd' name and awaken the 'living dead'. Our constituency had been born!

The rising popularity of the station was further multiplied by an unexpected episode. Lenka Wienerova, a Radio Stalin producer, remembers the story well.

> Even President Vaclav Havel decided to attend the Festival. When he arrived we asked him for an interview and he agreed. He was very kind, despite the physical circumstances; our studio was located in one of the cold, bad-smelling, damp pathways in the underground labyrinth. When we reached the studio, we asked the president to be seated in our only chair for the interview.

Public reaction to the interview was mostly positive; audiences understood it as a gesture of moral support for independent broadcasting. Nevertheless, some reactions were remonstrative, if not negative. For example, the most popular Czech weekly, *Mlady Svet* (The Young World), wrote:

> It is slightly striking that President Havel agreed to be interviewed by an illegal radio station. Regardless of whether the president agrees with the law, he should nevertheless abide by the existing law as a citizen, and also as the top representative of State.

The president felt called upon to react to the publicity and he did so with his usual diplomatic elegance and broadmindedness. In one of his regular Sunday afternoon chats for federal radio, he included a few words devoted to the Radio Stalin interview. He said that during his visit to the *Totalitarian Zone Festival* he was convinced by a group of nice young people to answer several questions for their station. He said that he had not known that the broadcast was not legally constituted. Nevertheless, he added, he thought there should be not only State-run stations, but independent ones as well.

Following the Vaclav interview on Friday, the station continued its Totalitarian Zone broadcasting until it received another official visitor.

> On Sunday, one of the local government officials came into our quarters and started to intimidate us, saying that we must immediately cease activities. He sat down in the same chair the president had used and eventually admitted, 'As a private citizen, I agree with your efforts, however, in my official capacity, I *must* comply with the law, and insist that you cease operations.'

Wienerova recalls that station personnel argued that since there was no law expressly forbidding independent broadcasts, the station could not be illegal. She doesn't know if the official accepted the argument, but the following Friday the police arrived at the station and seized the equipment.

We didn't see it again for several weeks, and we were even fined for the misdemeanour. Fortunately, we had chosen an unused frequency and not interfered with any other broadcasting, which had been the main argument against us. The legal proceedings against us were actually only symbolic.

Immediately after the episode with President Havel's interview, and after the seizing of the station equipment, a huge campaign in support of the right for independent broadcasting started. The Radio Stalin affair became a front-page event for several days in Czechoslovakian newspapers. It became a symbol not only of the struggle for freedom of expression in actual practice, but also the struggle for independent, non-commercial cultural activities. Protest petitions went to politicians, members of parliament, radio and television outlets and major newspapers. The spontaneously-established Union of Independent Broadcasting Applicants was heavily engaged in these efforts as well.

As a result of this campaign, the seized equipment was returned to Vladimir Vintr and his colleagues. TRS, a subsidiary of the Linhart Foundation, provided the station with a new headquarters in downtown Prague, directly across the river from the original site of broadcasting.

After the Velvet Revolution, Czech and Slovak cultural institutions, for years subsidized by government as propaganda tools, became free. But the threat of commercialization quickly developed. As for broadcasting, the immediate approval of a new broadcasting law by the Federal Parliament was of primary importance. It was proposed that independent broadcasters would receive a portion of the licence fees paid to the State by owners of radio and television receivers. Such a solution was expected to allow the non-State stations to act not only as commercially operated ones, but also to provide certain cultural services to the public. Lenka Wienerova recalls:

> In the first days of the year 1991, it became clear to everyone that the government would finally act. Subsequent to our proposal that the government issue temporary licenses to selected applicants, there were eight stations licensed in March. In the meantime, we decided to start again with our broadcasts from the new site, on the new frequency 91.9 FM. We changed our name from Radio Stalin to Radio Ultra, and now recently to Radio One. We were the first!

YOUTH RADIO

Most of the other new stations, including those outside of Prague that had been licensed later, did not begin operations until the Fall of 1991.

The State radio, for the first time in its history, had competitors, although it still had the trump cards: three nationwide networks (Federal,

Czech, and Slovak), several simultaneously operating programmes, ten regional studios and, most importantly, a government-secured budget. The Union of Independent Broadcasters required that a part of the fees paid by listeners went to the independent producers, reducing the government budget for State-run radio.

Now the new stations (for example: Radio RIO, Radio Plus, Radio Bonton, Radio Vox, Fun Radio) have to vie for listenership among themselves as well as against the State radio. Most of them are oriented toward "easy listening" programming, highlighting MOR formats. In this, there is the danger of homogenized sound, making it difficult for the listener to differentiate one station from another. The exception is Radio One. It has opted for its own specific programme philosophy and strictly serves the tastes of the younger generation.

Lenka Wienerova, now a producer at Radio One, says:

> We now employ eleven disc jockeys, all of whom had been volunteering their services until September, when we were able to begin providing them with salaries. They are absolutely free to choose the musical material and comment on it. All of them came from the underground music clubs and they have good sensitivity to their generation's desires. Their selection of programmatic material is authorized by their own personal tastes; if one likes Madonna, he or she plays Madonna with the conviction that others will like Madonna as well. We believe in a second value: we deplore indifference or indolence regarding the painful issues of our world. Therefore, we organize public events such as concerts supporting the Kurd nation, or the Czech National Library. During these events, we have a chance to meet our listeners, who are mainly highly educated youth of the city of Prague and its vicinities.
>
> Eighty-five per cent of our broadcasting time is devoted to music. Besides six-hour blocks of a disc jockey's time, our listeners are offered documentaries or special features dealing with lesser-known music, musicians, and styles. Three times weekly we schedule shorter presentations of classical music—opera, organ concerts, and devotional music—with accompanying explanations. A part of our log is our own 'hit parade', as well as an 'anti-parade'. We provide air time to the editors of two music journals.
>
> The rest of the schedule is filled with various interviews, reports, and commentaries broadcast under the title of *Pot-Pourri*. There is a

short news summary every hour; our news department consists of four editors.

We stopped paying the official Czechoslovak news agency (CTK) because its services were not compatible with our needs. Our information sources are: monitoring of other broadcasters, newspapers, and the services of the East European Information Agency (VIA). During dramatic world events, we invite the news editors of VIA to come to our studio for direct, live broadcasts. It was used, for example, during the U.S.S.R. 'coup' attempt in August 1991.

Hot news is broadcast immediately; we don't feel bound by any rules or regulations as do the news editors at the State radio. Twice a day, the English portion of the news is broadcast by the editors of *Prognosis*, the Prague-based English language newspaper.

HOW TO SURVIVE AND PROSPER

The big advantage enjoyed by Vintr's radio group was that they had the technical equipment at their disposal from the first moment of broadcasting. Nevertheless, the station is expensive to operate. Vladimir Vintr explains:

> Until September 1991, none of us received any salary whatsoever. Our commercial income was immediately reinvested. For the time being, we are able to cover about 25% of our costs with advertising revenue. We need to cover about 50% of our costs through it. After a year of broadcasting, we are realizing about 70-80% of our potential commercial revenue. Our prices are very reasonable, both because we understand that we are a community station and because we want to support smaller business ventures. Our licensing agency, TRS, borrowed millions of crowns from the bank. We receive some money from government, taken from listeners' licence fees. We intend, also, to borrow money from abroad, but we would like to stay independent in our decision-making. This is the only way that we can survive in an over-crowded ether in our broadcast area.

* * *

P.S.: According to the latest polls, from Winter 1991-1992, Radio One is now in third place in listenership in Prague!

21

Radyo Womanwatch

Anna Leah Sarabia

In the six years of its existence, Radyo Womanwatch has moved to four different radio stations. Moving has been one of the consequences of insisting on maintaining a public service and women's advocacy programme in a highly competitive commercial broadcast environment. Since the programme came to life in 1985 — as a women's programme, an advocacy programme and a public service programme rolled into one hour of talk, poetry, news and music — we have found it difficult to find a permanent home station or time slot. Inevitably, the format had to change according to the image and audience of each station and the schedule the programme was assigned to.

The first six months of Radyo Womanwatch were also the last six months of the regime of Ferdinand Marcos. The programme was broadcast over a government-run AM station in Metro Manila, DZFM-AM. (The FM in the station's call letters stood for Ferdinand Marcos. Another Manila station, DWIM-FM, had the initials of both Imelda and Ferdinand Marcos). Because the entire broadcast media industry was beholden to the Marcos government from the time Martial Law was declared in 1972 up to the twilight of the Marcos years in February 1986, it didn't seem to matter much whether a talk show was aired on a private station or a government station. In fact, using the official propaganda arm provided a good "cover," since DZFM was controlled media and therefore not as closely watched by the military as private stations were. The other advantage was that it cost us nothing to air the programme. The entire Bureau of Broadcasts, which ran DZFM, was amply provided for by the National Budget, and needed no advertising or extra income from "blocktimers" like us. As with many government run agencies in the Philippines, knowing someone "up there" helped. The station manager was my cousin, and that helped when we presented our case.

Imelda Marcos had been professing official concern for women's issues ever since 1975, when she headed the Philippine delegation to the World Conference on Women in Mexico. But it was not until after the assassination of Marcos' arch rival Ninoy Aquino in 1983 that middle class and grassroots women organized and that hundreds of new women's groups began to assert themselves as a potent political force and insisted that women's issues be put onto the agenda. The print media had noticed this growing force, especially since it was women journalists and columnists that first dared to openly criticize the Marcos authority in print. The broadcast media, however, recognized only Imelda Marcos, her daughter, and women officials of the government, as the nation's female political leaders.

It was in this situation that Radyo Womanwatch, the first women's advocacy programme in the country, took its first tentative steps. We were allowed to go on the air, but under the following conditions: that we did not criticize the First Family and the favourite government officials, and that we did not promote anti-government sentiments. We could discuss rape and violence against women in general terms, but we could not discuss military rape or human rights violations. We could denounce the spread of sexually-transmitted diseases in areas around the US military bases, but we could not talk about the sex tour promotions of the Department of Tourism. We could criticize the movie industry for promoting soft core pornography, but we could not address "first daughter" Imee Marcos' use of public funds to promote so-called "art films."

Nevertheless, we felt that there was enough room to move. Sexism in the workplace, women's health, creativity, religious and cultural prejudice, migrant workers, teenage pregnancy — there was a lot to talk about.

We were fascinated with our new found forum. For the first time, the three organizations which founded the programme — the Women's Desk of the Concerned Artists of the Philippines, the Progressive Women's Spiritual Association, and Filipina — were addressing audiences we did not see, did not know, and could not count. We were using "high-tech" facilities that we always thought would be beyond our reach. And we were getting the cooperation of women professionals on a volunteer basis. Even within a government station, Womanwatch was able to participate in the anti-Marcos movement. The great urge to change the system was manifest in the number of people and the manner through which they came together in those days to work, to protest and to invent alternative expressions. In our own group, only the anchor woman was paid a transportation allowance, because it was the only thing she did for a living. The rest of us made do as we could and devoted whatever free time we had to the programme.

Gertie Tirona, a historian who joined the Women's Media Circle some years later, has studied the period of our organization's birth. She wrote:

> To go back in time, 1985 was the worst and the best of years for the Philippine women's movement. Political repression took its toll of lives and limbs only to fuel patriotic fervour to fever pitch. It led to the birth of rainbow coalitions and a broad spectrum of organizations of concerned women. Though many of the game activists who went live on radio in a spontaneous outpouring of enthusiasm are relatively young, already memories begin to dim when asked to recount their salad days on Radyo Womanwatch.
>
> The casual air, the happenstance posture, the healthy exuberance, the penniless past, the anonymity — ingredients that do not make a show in the fiercely competitive and star-studded Philippine broadcast and television industry — are among their noteworthy recollections. Even they can now reflect in amazement that a programme can be so informally hatched...
>
> Seen in retrospect, it seems uncanny that this (first day of broadcast, October 27, 1985) was also the eve of what is now celebrated by the Filipino women's movement as their Day of Protest, when a united front of thousands of women from all classes, sectors and regions converged...to stage an indignation rally against the Marcos regime in 1983.

But it was not without difficulties that Radyo Womanwatch, and the Women's Media Circle, managed to survive. We existed on the generosity of family and friends, who were willing to donate some money for the purchase of tapes, or bake a few loaves of sweet bread for post-recording snacks. We raised taxi fare for guest poets among ourselves, and guests who could afford to, contributed financially and morally.

Ironically, the onset of the Aquino government made us realize our vulnerability. With the fall of Marcos, the management of almost all major broadcasting networks in Manila changed hands. The Bureau of Broadcast (BB), as well as the entire Department of Public Information, was abandoned, for all intents and purposes, by everyone from the top directors to the technicians. It took two weeks for the People Power takeover of the BB and GTV-4, the Government Television Channel, to settle down. In the chaos, however, we had to speak to half a dozen people, hoping that, with the lack of producers and programmes to transmit, the new managers would give us the opportunity to continue Radyo Womanwatch. They did. Through the transition period, and for another year, the programme went on — first, under the newly organized Radyo ng Bayan (Peoples' Radio), and then back to DZFM, rehabilitated as Sports Radio.

Funding the programme was becoming a problem though, because all the volunteers had to earn a living. In our sixth month of broadcast, a nun working with migrant workers, who we interviewed on the programme, taught us how to write out project proposals for funding grants. With this new-found knowledge, we proceeded to write to several funding agencies. Two responded positively: the Asia Foundation, which had an office in Manila, and the Spanish organization, Manos Unidas. Twelve months after we recorded the first programme, Radyo Womanwatch finally became financially viable. We were able to purchase a field microphone, a tape recorder, some cassettes and open reel tapes, and to give ourselves, the guests, and the technicians, a small allowance.

But the perils of producing a radio programme on the basis of other people's kindness soon were manifest. Kindness is a limited resource in such a highly competitive industry as media, and when this resource is demanded by persons and agencies more powerful than ours (government forums or sports events), projects like Radyo Womanwatch must be pushed aside — in broadcast terms, must be "pre-empted." By 1988 the Aquino government was becoming less generous with its airtime for "outsiders" like us, no matter that we were among the activists who helped recover the facilities from the Marcos minions during the People's Revolt. How could we build an audience if our programme had no regularity?

At the time we were sharing precious resources with other women's groups, offering them portions of our weekly hour for their own features and interviews. Our contributions, however, did not go unnoticed, and in 1989 we were able to secure support from the Asian Partnership for Human Development (APHD), a Catholic organization based in Hong Kong. Through a grant from them, we were able to move out of the Bureau of

Broadcasts and buy airtime from a better rated "sequestered" (i.e. formerly Marcos controlled but now Aquino monitored) commercial AM station, DWAN.

In our tradition of participatory production, we invited six women's organizations to take turns producing Radyo Womanwatch with us. Thus we had Professor Tirona of the Women's Studies Consortium, poet Marra Lanot of the Concerned Artists of the Philippines, Petite Peredo of Gabriela, counsellor Reena Marcelo of the Institute for Social Studies and Action, Princess Nemenzo of the Women's Health Coalition, and rural women organizer Trining Domingo of the KaBaPa (Movement of Progressive Women). We met with them every two months to plan themes and topics together with the main anchor, Sonia Capio, an experienced broadcaster who spent much time during the Marcos era interviewing opposition leaders in a political talk show that finally had to close down due to lack of funds. For all of us, the challenge was how best to make use of each broadcast hour to reach out to women — we went on the air in the mornings of Monday, Wednesday and Friday. During these meetings, we shared learning experiences, discussed interaction with guests and audiences, and assessed the successes or failures of our format.

By the time our one year contract with DWAN ended, in 1990, Radyo Womanwatch had been cited as "Best Informational Program" by the Catholic Mass Media Awards. This award was the first any programme of DWAN had won, and encouraged the station managers to renew our contract at a discounted rate for another six months. It also gave us the temerity to find another grant for the programme before the APHD money ran out. Before the contract ended, however, the station was taken over by an Aquino associate, who changed the station from one with a political and public service image into a 100% entertainment, gossip and "good news" format. Since none of us were stars or tabloid columnists, Radyo Womanwatch had to go.

Our next, and current home is at a newly reprogrammed station, DWIZ, which is aggressively pursuing a public affairs profile, and moving to the top five in Metro Manila a.m. ratings. Radyo Womanwatch now goes on the air every evening for half an hour (7:00 to 7:30 p.m.). From Monday to Thursday, Sonia Capio handles *Womanwatch Action Line* which focuses on political leadership, environment, art and culture, labour and other related topics. When we launched the new Radyo Womanwatch last November, we also began airing *Womanwatch Healthline* which aims at a young adult audience and focuses on health, relationships and the prevention of teenage pregnancy. Research, planning and part-time staffing for this programme are provided by the Institute for Social Studies and Action and the Women's Health Care Foundation.

So far, it is the most successful format we have produced for radio, but it is also the most expensive. We have funding in place to cover the basics for the next year, provided by three foundations. We are also trying to generate some additional revenue from advertising, and a few companies have responded with interest, if not signed contracts. However, money is a constant worry and we still have to raise some from a variety of sources to cover a portion of our production costs.

Of course, we will not give up hope of one day setting up our own radio cooperative outside of Metro Manila, in a province where women can make use of the airwaves to empower themselves. Recent changes in National Telecommunication Commission policy may make it easier to get a license, and make it possible for us to finally set up our dream home base, Radyo ag Kababaihan (Women's Radio). In the meantime, we take each opportunity as it comes, and use the airwaves so that women may somehow be uplifted.

* * *

22

Making waves with CASET

Edric Gorfinkel

The Cassette Education Trust (CASET) is a community service project based in the Salt River industrial area of Cape Town, South Africa. The project was established in 1989 to "develop the usefulness of audio-cassette as a medium of communication in the struggle for a sustainable democracy." Because broadcasting was State-controlled, CASET produced and distributed audio-cassette programmes, which in more open circumstances would be broadcast on radio. Another emphasis was the creation of a training ground for future broadcasters.

By February 1992, as a result of the changing political climate in South Africa and the Conference for a Democratic South Africa (CODESA) negotiations, CASET, together with Bush Radio (a broad-based community radio initiative), was on the verge of going on air as part of a legally constituted community broadcasting sector.

The following collage tells the story of CASET and the emerging community radio movement through an assemblage of historical notes, CASET documents, and exerpts from an interview with the project's founder and coordinator, Edric Gorfinkel, conducted by Diarmuid McLean.

* * *

THE TALKING NEWSPAPER PILOT PROJECT

February 1988: The Talking Newspaper Pilot project (TNPP) is suggested as a testing ground for using audio-cassettes as a mass medium of communication. The TNPP is conducted in the midst of a nationwide State of Emergency including a media "blackout." It is not an easy time to launch a new media project, so a couple of "smokescreens" are set up to make it appear innocuous. Firstly it is articulated as "providing access to the print media for people with handicaps to independent reading (visual impairment and illiteracy)." Secondly it is made to look like an academic exercise by couching the study in the context of the University of Cape Town's Community Adult Education Programme (CAEP).

From CAEP Project Outline — February 1988, *Audio-Cassette as an Appropriate Education Medium:*

- Communication (or the lack of it) lies close to the heart of the conflict that is South Africa. As the conflict deepens, communication is stifled. We need to be constantly exploring not only new ways of using media, but also using new media.
- The print media are well used (given government restrictions). Video is becoming increasingly accessible to more sections of the community. On the other hand radio and TV are State controlled.
- Popular video is to television, as the audio-cassette is to radio — the appropriate technology equivalent.
- By producing cassette programmes we could open an entirely new area of the media to popular use.
- Everyone has a tape recorder, or easy access to one, but they're used almost exclusively for listening to music. Blind people use them in more varied ways, to listen to novels, theatre, stories etc.. However, producing material still seems to be in the hands of very few people.
- It can be very easy to produce cassettes. On one level, one person can speak into one microphone, record it and make copies on just about any modern hi-fi equipment. On another level a communal studio could synthesize input from a network of sources and reproduce those programmes for popular distribution.

Edric: I worked with the Zimbabwe Broadcasting Corporation (ZBC) for a few years while I was exiled from South Africa. This experience had a direct influence on what I hoped to accomplish with CASET. Very little had been done there before independence to prepare progressive people to take over the radio and television services. So at the time of independence, and still today in fact, there are die-hard Rhodesians producing radio programmes, doing a lot that is not in the national interest. But they stay there because there's no one to replace them.

Listeners still have a negative attitude towards the ZBC. The whole issue of control and ownership is fundamental to people's attitudes towards that radio station.

If you had somebody you wanted to interview for ZBC, the effort to get those people to actually talk when the tape was turning around, my god! They were always so guarded about it because they didn't trust the ZBC. It was a dreaded thing to go on the air. It wasn't an exciting thing.

That's what gave me the idea of saying we have to have people in control.

South Africa is divided up by Group Areas and by apartheid legislation. This separates people out so it is very difficult for us to meet physically. The radio template could establish links that could get people talking to each other again. That's not happening now.

The neo-Nazi thugs, parading in khaki, fucking up their servants and massacring their families — they need healing. The township *laaitie*[1] who's been shot at by *mabulu,*[2] has watched a necklace and his dreams are full of broken images — we all need healing in this country. We have to talk to each other. It's not enough that just the leaders are doing it.

I wanted to do radio, but I wanted to do a particular kind of radio.

CASET *(THE CASSETTE EDUCATION TRUST)*

June 1988: With most of the material for the Talking Newspapers being drawn from the independent weekly newspapers, listener feedback immediately prompts an increasing in the amount of "live" sound on the programmes. Community organisations and activists become the primary target audience. Over the next year, with growing support for the project from progressive organisations and a rising tide of defiance against the repressive Botha/Malan regime, it is decided that an audio-cassette service organisation should be set up: the CASsette Education Trust (CASET).

From the CASET Brochure — June 1989, *Audio-Cassette: The Appropriate Technology Equivalent of Radio:*

> Everybody knows them, many people own them, most people use them in taxis and cars, in classrooms and fac-

> tories, at work and at home audio-cassette is already a mass medium mostly for listening to music, but it can be used to popularize a lot more than music: poetry, story-telling and oral histories; speeches, debates, sermons and lectures; interviews, discussions and conferences; drama, children's songs and indigenous music; news analysis, topical issues or a talking newspaper.
>
> The State still controls radio and TV, but it cannot control audio-cassette. Given the legacy of systematic disempowerment through State control of information, we need to use any medium of communication that is accessible to the struggle for a free, united and healthy South Africa.

June 1989: Funding for the first year of CASET is secured from the Scottish Catholic International Aid Fund (SCIAF). Premises are chosen, equipment purchased, offices established and work begins. "People's poet" Sandile Dikeni is trained to produce programmes.

The project is guided and supervised by a Board of Trustees. The Trustees are respected members of the community, all of them with an interest in education or media. They include a Muslim theologian and leading figure in the democratic movement, a musician, a librarian, an oral historian, a photo-journalist renowned for his coverage of the struggle against apartheid, and a professor of Afrikaans literature committed to the "People's Education" movement.

October 1989: A mass campaign of defiance is triggered by the so-called "last racist elections" — P.W. Botha's last ditch attempt to legitimate a racially-based constitution. This Defiance Campaign, the second in the history of the struggle against apartheid, is destined to bring down the Botha/Malan junta and heralds the dawn of de Klerk's "new" South Africa. It takes another two years before opponents get to the negotiating table. This is the period of CASET's operation, hitting the streets with the Defiance Campaign.

Edric: Another tricameral election and massive opposition to it. Obviously there is a story brewing and press from all over the world pulls into town. Peace March in Cape Town, mass rallies in St. George's Cathedral, organisations unbanning themselves... Hot news for the BBC kinda stuff. This is a big story, so we say let's go, let's go pick up this stuff. Getting the speeches, vox popping people, recording the *toyi-toyi.*[3]

The response from the activist organisers was, "Great idea, let's go, this is gonna be an important new medium. We can spread this thing around. People in rural areas can hear what they weren't able to attend."

But vox popping was something people on the street were completely unaccustomed to. Nobody had ever asked them their opinions. The foreign journalists filmed them from afar, but they didn't talk to them that much. Each time we talked to somebody we'd tell them that we were going to produce an audio-cassette for distribution amongst community organizations.

There'd been a tradition of "agents provocateurs," infiltrating the movement, so it helped that a lot of people knew us. We would not have been able to do the same thing in Port Elizabeth or Durban. Because it was in Cape Town we were able to go ahead. People who were organizing the events knew us and that was the reference point for a lot of their involvement.

The programme was a cooperative production with the United Democratic Front (UDF) although they were a restricted organisation. Initially the agreement was that we'd make seven copies, and those seven tapes would go to the seven branches of the UDF in the Western Cape area. On the basis of their feedback we were to decide where the programme would go and how to distribute it.

However, because of the nature of events at that time, those seven tapes went out to the branches but there was never a coordinated meeting to discuss what would happen to the programme after that. So we didn't distribute any other tapes. There were only those seven tapes, but that programme reached the whole country. People just made copies. Some people arrived here and said to us, "We believe you made this tape," and put it on. It was something like a 10th generation copy!

July 1989: The recording of conferences, which become a feature of the "new" South Africa, is one of the primary income generating services of CASET. Most conference recordings are archived as an accurate record of proceedings, transcribed for print publications, or copied in full for wider listenership. Some, like the Institute for a Democratic Alternative in South Africa (IDASA)/ANC Writers' Conference at the Victoria Falls in Zimbabwe, result in the production of audio programmes.

Edric: The Defiance Campaign was just beginning to brew. The ANC was still a banned organisation. There were a lot of ANC safaris organised by

IDASA and a lot of government harrasment of people when they returned to the country. The Victoria Falls conference organizers wanted to have the proceedings recorded and transcribed for a book. We said to them, "We're not going to charge you for this. You just pay for our transport, and we'll produce programmes from it."

For three hours, the poetry evening brought together one of the most representative and exciting groups of South African poets. It was incredible. People like Willie Kgositsile and Breyten Breytenbach, Antjie Krog, Wally Serote, Ingrid de Kock, Hein Willemse (who's also a CASET Trustee now)...really amazing people.

So we produced one tape of poetry — *Musi oa Tunye:*[4] Poetry that Thunders; another one of prose and story telling, with Vernie Februarie and Albie Sachs, and then another one which included some of the conference itself — Breyten Breytenbach's *Is my writing part of South African literature?*, (speaking mainly to the Afrikaners), and then Willie Kgositsile's talk about *The role of the exiled writer in the struggle for national liberation.* They're good friends, they've got a similar style of speaking, story-telling, and there's lots of resonant themes in what they talk about. So we put that and their poetry on two sides of a tape.

The Defiance Campaign and similar material was far more politically agitational, whereas the *Musi oa Tunye* tapes were more culturally reflective.

At the same time as this was going on, Sandile was producing a whole lot of other things: *Stop the Hangings,* about capital punishment; *On Local Government,* about the role of local government in negotiations; *Unban SANSCO* (South African National Students Organization), produced for and with the organisation, using their people and their material.

We were also introducing people to radio and training them to produce programmes. We did some *Ghettoblaster Workshops* which involved taking some blank tapes and a double-cassette machine to wherever people were meeting anyway, and doing a three hour workshop. Recording whatever people wanted to do: songs, stories, interviews etc. You edit that stuff on a double-deck and produce a programme. Then you can make copies. That technique was successful in giving people a feel for participatory community radio. The quality's not that great, but people dig just hearing themselves "play radio."

Three ways of distributing tapes developed because of different situations. Sometimes people made lots and lots of copies. That was exciting, when it just ran away with itself. Secondly, we sold tapes, like *ANC Speaks* and *Mandela Speaks,* which were also copied. Thirdly, we would produce a programme with a particular organization and they would handle their own distribution. There's no doubt that informal copying by organizations and individuals reached far more people than selling tapes did.

In South Africa, if people spend money to buy a tape, they're really committed. The people who were the most committed were the people who were most politically active, so as a result the most political tapes sold best. We did a whole series of tapes which were political education seminars on various issues. Those are programmes we constantly have a call for.

But without a doubt, the most popular programmes are the music tapes, *Chorimba* and *Freedom Sings.*

AN OPENING FOR COMMUNITY RADIO

February 1990: A dramatic about face on the part of the new de Klerk administration, unbanning liberation movements and releasing Nelson Mandela from thirty years in prison, sets a new context for the agendas of democratic organizations. CASET is catapulted into addressing its long-term objective: the transformation of broadcasting in South Africa.

Traditionally monopolized by the State, broadcasting has not been on the agenda of the democratic movement other than FAWO's (The Film and Allied Workers Organization) work on broadcasting as a constitutional issue, and the work of the ANC's Radio Freedom. Broadcasting from exile in other African countries to a listenership largely denied access to shortwave receivers, Radio Freedom's programmes are also known through their distribution on audio-cassettes.

Now the unbanning of liberation movements and the release of political prisoners begins to open up political activity inside the country. The return of exiled broadcasters provides fresh impetus for the emerging debates around the future of radio and TV. A growing body of democratic organizations inside the country begin to look at how they can use the broadcast media, mounting a wave of protest against the government controlled South African Broadcasting Corporation (SABC). This enables CASET to focus attention on developing its vision for community radio.

Edric: I really did think that audio-cassette could be the appropriate technology equivalent of radio, but it just isn't. Publishing stuff on audio-cassette is more like publishing a book than it is like doing radio. Its greatest potential lies as an aid to formal education, distance learning together with visual packages, maps, comics, readings et cetera. There's still a lot of experimenting to be done with audio-cassette.

There should've been pirate radio in South Africa, and there wasn't! The whole approach we're taking is to say, "let's go the legislative route. Change the whole society and community radio will make sense." In other parts of the world they tried to change the radio while the society stayed the same, so community radio is marginal in those places. I don't see why community radio should be marginal. Community organization has been central to the process of social change in South Africa. Community radio must be as central.

Part of the work that CASET has been doing is to make people more aware of the importance of radio. The result (not only of CASET's efforts but a lot of other people's efforts as well), is that broadcasting is on the negotiations agenda. It is now recognized by all political parties that it must come under independent control. I would say that CASET has contributed significantly to making that a priority.

South Africa has twenty-seven radio stations and at least four television channels. It's got one of the best transmitter networks anywhere in the world, let alone Africa, and an external broadcasting capacity that can cover the whole world. I think it is really important who has access to those facilties.

One of CASET's main activities was training and getting people prepared for eventual access to the airwaves. But this creates its own problems. What are you training for? Community radio or audio-cassette? Training revolves around concrete, usable programmes. The people who are producing a *Talking Newsletter* on tape, for example, are constantly learning and growing because they're using their skills all the time. But we said we were using audio-cassette to train for community radio, which still doesn't exist. There's nowhere to plug people in once they've been trained.

November 1990: New CASET staffmember Hein Marais, returning from Canada with experience of Community Radio, presents an important paper on Community Radio to a national media conference. This firmly places the issue of community radio on the national agenda. A series of subsequent conferences, workshops and seminars builds wide-ranging support for the idea of a community radio sector, understood as being a natural extension of South Africa's powerful democratic community organisations.

From the Conclusion of: *Talking Back — the Case for Community Radio* by Hein Marais — November 1990:

> We are entering — and in many respects are already in — a period marked by the constant propagation, in fact the aggressive marketing of a new, normalized South Africa. Few need to be reminded that there is little that is "normal" about South African society, nor are we likely to experience this blessed state of affairs in the foreseeable future.
>
> This "selling of normality" is probably the prime ideological feature of this country today...It is a dangerous tendency, in the sense that it does not so much challenge or confront reality as it seeks to transcend or leap over reality and replace it with an imagined state of affairs. It is complicit in the strongest degree with this collective amnesia into which so many South Africans are so fast retreating.
>
> The paramount task of progressive media is to rupture this artificial construct of normality; it is to break this imagined consensus about who we are and to what we aspire.
>
> Needless to say, I believe Community Radio can play a role in helping to accomplish this task.

March 1991: In a public meeting CASET proposes a community radio network to community organizations in Cape Town. The proposal is well received and results in a series of monthly open forums in the name of Bush Radio. The initial idea of locating the radio station at the University of the Western Cape (known as the People's Campus) is gradually overturned by community organizations because of the danger of rarifying community participation.

Raging debates in the Bush Radio Open Forums, together with regular meetings of an elected Coordinating Committee, become watershed work in the emerging community radio movement in South Africa. Other initiatives start up in other parts of the country, notably Durban and Grahamstown. The presence of Radio Freedom, now relocating in Johannesburg, adds fuel to the fire. A group of South Africans on a community radio training programme in Canada adds to the pool of committed community radio activists.

January 1992: As CODESA emerges from its first session, a high-powered conference on Media in Transition is called by COM (Campaign for Open Media) to make resolutions to the relevant CODESA Working Group.

CASET convenes a pre-conference meeting on community radio which drafts a Resolution on Community Radio. The resolution emphasizes the importance of an independent broadcasting authority and of community broadcasting, and calls for an equitable distribution of resources to public, commercial and community radio. The resolution is adopted by the Conference.

February 1992: In addition, the general Resolution on the Electronic Media reserves spectrum space for community-based broadcasting and proposes a Communications Development Fund to finance it. At the time of writing, these resolutions are with the relevant CODESA Working Group. The distinct possibility of community radio licenses being issued within the next six months brings into sharp relief the years of groundwork done by CASET and Bush Radio. Popular pressure to go on the air can be met, but the political expedience of doing so immediately is still a subject of debate.

From Bush Radio Open Forum Minutes — February 1992, *On Air Proposal:*

> Most of our difficulties can be put down to having no prior experience of community radio broadcasting. It was therefore proposed that we start broadcasting as soon as possible! We have the means. This would of course mean that we are pirating the airwaves, which is illegal, but it may be the only way to conscientise people about community radio. There is no guarantee we will get a license through CODESA. If we go on air we will be much more difficult to ignore. There are lots of issues to be considered around this proposal and it needs to be discussed by organizations who must decide if they would support such a move. This could be treated as a training and test phase. If we do get stopped it could become a public issue, and we could spark a campaign of defiance involving other community radio initiatives.

From Bush Radio Open Forum Minutes — March 1992, *On Air Proposal:*

> Debate around whether we should go on the air immediately ran along two basic lines. The one was to say: "we're just about to get licenses anyway so why run the risk of fines, jail and equipment loss at this stage of negotiations?." The other line was: "we've been saying that for years. Civics without electricity don't stop fighting for it because of negotiations...."
>
> It was felt that we should prepare a comprehensive "switch-on campaign" including license applications to both the Minister of Home Affairs and to CODESA/ICA. The Grahamstown Workshop could be used to facilitate a national campaign. If we exhaust all avenues for legal permission to go on the air, we can show that we are being unjustly treated by regulatory authorities, and are confident of broad-based popular support — only then should we consider broadcasting in defiance of legalities. It was however noted that this should not stall efforts to make small, cheap transmitters available for community use.

From the Jabulani! Freedom of the Airwaves conference, *The Future of Radio in South Africa* — Don Pinnock:

> By way of conclusion let me say this: Radio is a way to bring the sounds of all Africa to the south — sounds which apartheid has held back from our ears for so long. It is a way to start building what Albie Sachs calls "a rainbow culture,"[5] where Marabi music and Mozart jostle for airtime with T.S. Elliot and Mzwakhe Mbuli. Where Tolstoy and Todd Matshikize share the same waveband and where people start to dismantle group areas in their hearts.
>
> We have hardly begun to explore the beauty of our many cultures with the microphone, and we need to make a start now.

Edric: Listen, there's a lot of things CASET didn't do. And a lot of things we shouldn't have done, or should have done differently. There's a hell of a lot more that could still be done with audio-cassettes and I hope other people will pick it up. Little CASET can't do everything! We set out to get the voice of the people on the air and by the time this lands on the pages of a book we probably will be on the air. CASET has set up a broadcast studio and a whole office infrastructure. Together with the Bush Radio people we've got a really interesting, dynamic democratic process going that could be a real case of grassroots development — warts and all!

* * *

NOTES

1. laaitie: lighty, youngster.
2. mabulu: boers, security police and soldiers.
3. toyi-toyi: a protest rally incorporating dancing and singing
4. Musi oa Tunye: "the smoke that thunders," the indigenous Zimbabwean name for the Victoria Falls.
5. Former Archbishop Desmond Tutu first coined the phrase "rainbow culture": a culture of all colours.

COMMON CENTS

Media Portrayal of the Gulf War and Other Events

James Winter

Using eight crucial case studies, ranging from the Gulf War, to Oka, the Ontario NDP budget, and the Montréal Massacre, James Winter shows how media coverage of events consistently casts them in what becomes a 'common-sense' framework—a framework that tends to undermine the broader public interest while underwriting a narrowly-defined, allegedly "national interest", which actually represents the power elite.

Common Cents documents, in painstaking detail, how, and why, the media use this power to reinforce neoconservative views, with devastating ramifications for discourse in society, and democracy itself.

220 pages
Paperback ISBN: 1-895431-24-7 $19.95
Hardcover ISBN: 1-895431-25-5 $38.95
Communications/Current Events/Canadian Studies

BEYOND HYPOCRISY

Decoding the News in an Age of Propaganda

Including a Doublespeak Dictionary for the 1990s

Edward S. Herman

Illustrations by Matt Wuerker

In a highly original volume that includes an extended essay on the Orwellian use of language that characterizes U.S. political culture, cartoons, and a cross-referenced lexicon of *doublespeak* terms with examples of their all too frequent usage, Herman and Wuerker highlight the deception and hypocrisy contained in the U.S. government's favourite buzzwords. This spirited book offers abundant examples of duplicitous terminology, ranging from the crimes of free enterprise celebrated in the boardrooms of Wall Street and the press coverage of elections in El Salvador and Nicaragua to George Bush's condemnation of Saddam Hussein's invasion of Kuwait – after having just indulged in similarly straightforward aggression in Panama only one year previously.

Edward S. Herman is Professor of Finance at the Wharton School, University of Pennsylvania. A columnist for *Z Magazine,* he has written a number of books on foreign policy and mass media – *The Real Terror Network,* and with Noam Chomsky, *The Political Economy of Human Rights,* both of which have been published by **Black Rose Books.**

204 pages, illustrations, index
Paperback ISBN: 0-895431-48-4 $19.95
Hardcover ISBN: 0-895431-49-2 $38.95
International Politics/Sociology/Communications

FROM THE GROUND UP

Essays on Grassroots and Workplace Democracy

C. George Benello

Edited by Len Krimerman, Frank Lindenfeld, Carol Korty & Julian Benello

Foreword by Dimitrios Roussopoulos

Should today's activists aim for more than reformist changes in the policies and personnel of giant corporations and the government? In this collection of classic essays, C. George Benello persuasively argues that modern social movements need to rise to the challenge of spearheading a radical reorganization of society based on the principles of decentralization, community control, and participatory democracy. Integrating some of the best of New Left thought with more contemporary populist and Green perspectives, Benello's essays and the commentaries of Harry Boyte, Steve Chase, Walda Katz-Fishman, Jane Mansbridge and Chuck Turner offer important insights for today's new generation of practical utopians.

*Where the utopian confronts the practical, Benello is perhaps most creative...*From the Ground Up*...is a valuable contribution to creating a new politics.*
Z Magazine

C. George Benello, active in the movement for grassroots and workplace democracy from the early 1960s until his death in 1987, founded the Federation for Economic Democracy, the Industrial Cooperative Association, and the journal *Changing Work*.

251 pages, index
Paperback ISBN: 1-895431-32-8 **$19.95**
Hardcover ISBN: 1-895431-33-6 **$38.95**
Sociology/Politics

VIDEO THE CHANGING WORLD

Edited by Nancy Thede & Alain Ambrosi

An international collection of articles explore the variety of initiatives that have emerged the world over in the past decade, the challenges they face in making their voices heard, as well as the internal debates and problems that must be resolved in order to move towards a true democratization of video and television.

224 pages
Paperback ISBN: 0-895431-02-6 **$18.95**
Hardcover ISBN: 0-921689-03-4 **$37.95**
LC No. 91-72979
Communications

FIGHTING FOR HOPE

Organizing to Realize Our Dreams

Joan Newman Kuyek

Fighting For Hope *delivers an important message: that we can ourselves initiate change.*
Peace and Environment News

Kuyek provides a valuable list of do's and don'ts for social justice activists, and her emphasis on building structures for self-reliant communities is important for today's victims of recession. Her personal experience stories are rich and evocative.
Calgary Herald

As economic development—free-enterprise style—has progressed, its corollary has been the pillage not only of natural resources but of natural relationships. *Fighting For Hope* begins with an analysis of these forces and the ways in which resistance against them has been managed and suppressed. Activists in Canada have experienced dismal setbacks, unexpected victories and carefully planned successes. This book finds the common threads and weaves them into a guidebook for anyone who cares about social change.

Joan Newman Kuyek is the author of *The Phone Book: Working at Bell Canada, Managing the Household: A Handbook For Economic Justice Work,* and numerous articles and pamphlets.

209 pages
Paperback ISBN: 0-921689-86-1 $16.95
Hardcover ISBN: 0-921689-87-X $35.95
Politics/Sociology/Social Work

COMMUNICATION

For and Against Democracy

Edited by Marc Raboy and Peter A. Bruck

These pieces...do much to increase reader awareness of the increasing "mediatization" of society, the role of communications in global politics and economics, social experimentation with communication practices in national settings, and the strenghts and limitation of mass communication instruments as "facilitators of democracy"...a readable blend of descriptive material and critical viewpoints.
Choice

248 pages
Paperback ISBN: 0-921689-46-2 $19.95
Hardcover ISBN: 0-921689-47-0 $39.95
Communications

Black Rose Books has also published the following books of related interests:

Dissidence: Essays Against the Mainstream, *by Dimitrios Roussopoulos*
From Camp David to the Gulf: Negotiations, Language and Propaganda, and War, *by Adel Safty*
Language and Politics, *by Noam Chomsky*
Radical Priorities, *by Noam Chomsky, edited by C.P. Otero*
The Culture of Terrorism, *by Noam Chomsky*
The Fateful Triangle, *by Noam Chomsky*
On Power and Ideology, *by Noam Chomsky*
Pirates and Emperors: International Terrorism in the Real World, *by Noam Chomsky*
The Politics of Human Rights: Volume 1, The Washington Connection and Third World Fascism, *by Noam Chomsky*
The Politics of Human Rights: Volume 2, After the Cataclysm: Postwar Indochina and the Reconstruction of Imperial Ideology, *by Noam Chomsky*
Turning the Tide: The US and Latin America, *by Noam Chomsky*
Bureaucracy and Community, *edited by Linda Davies and Eric Shragge*
Community Action: Organizing for Social Change, *by Henri Lamoureux, Robert Mayer, and Jean Panet-Raymond*

Send for our free catalogue of books
BLACK ROSE BOOKS
C.P. 1258, Succ. Place du Parc
Montréal, Québec
H2W 2R3 Canada

Printed by
the workers of
Editions Marquis, Montmagny, Québec
for
Black Rose Books Ltd.